(((SEMITISM)))

(((SEMITISM)))

Being Jewish in America
in the Age of Trump

Jonathan Weisman

St. Martin's Press
New York

www.stmartins.com

Library of Congress Cataloging-in-Publication Data
Names: Weisman, Jonathan, author.
Title: (((Semitism))) : being Jewish in America in the age of Trump / Jonathan Weisman.
Description: First edition. | New York : St. Martin's Press, [2017] | Includes index.
Identifiers: LCCN 2017043692 | ISBN 9781250169938 (hardcover) | ISBN 9781250169945 (ebook)
Subjects: LCSH: Antisemitism—United States—History—21st century. | Trump, Donald, 1946- | Religious right—United States. | United States—Politics and government—21st century. | Jews—United States—History—21st century. | Jews—United States—Ethnic relations. | Jews—United States—Public opinion.
Classification: LCC DS146.U6 W45 2018 | DDC 305.892/4073—dc23
LC record available at https://lccn.loc.gov/2017043692

Our books may be purchased in bulk for promotional, educational, or business use. Please contact your local bookseller or the Macmillan Corporate and Premium Sales Department at 1-800-221-7945, extension 5442, or by email at MacmillanSpecialMarkets@macmillan.com.

First Edition: March 2018

10 9 8 7 6 5 4 3 2 1

To Jennifer

Contents

You shall appoint magistrates and officials for your tribes, in all the settlements that the Lord your God is giving you, and they shall govern the people with due justice. You shall not judge unfairly: you shall show no partiality; you shall not take bribes, for bribes blind the eyes of the discerning and upset the plea of the just. Justice, justice shall you pursue, that you may thrive and occupy the land that the Lord your God is giving you.

Deut. 16:18–20

(((SEMITISM)))

Introduction

On a pleasant June day in 2017, two groups of mostly young men, maybe a hundred or so, gathered in separate spots in the nation's capital. The new president of the United States was on Twitter, railing against his tormentors like a defenseless victim rather than the most powerful man in the world. The investigation of alleged collusion between Trump associates and Russian intelligence during the 2016 campaign was quietly gaining steam. Trump's political agenda was stymied, his approval ratings at remarkable lows for someone who had been in office for only half a year. But all was not lost for the forty-fifth president. In society at large, far beyond 1600 Pennsylvania Avenue, a new force was taking hold, at least in part in the president's name—one that was allowing bigotry to break into the open without fear of censure or shame. On the contrary, a weird kind of heroism was taking shape in certain circles of the country—indeed, of the world—where "political incorrectness" was to be heralded, the more incorrect the better. Donald J. Trump was having an impact.

So it was that at the foot of the Lincoln Memorial, a site redolent with meaning, where Dr. Martin Luther King Jr. told the world of his dream and where Lincoln's second inaugural address warning that "every drop of blood drawn with the lash shall be paid by another drawn with the sword" is etched in marble, the leaders of what has become known as the alt-right stood before a hundred or so followers. They were clad in khakis and white polo shirts—the Brownshirts of our time—and they cheered as the men (and one woman) at the microphone spewed anti-immigrant, racist, and anti-Semitic free speech. At the same time, in front of Trump's White House, a smaller group, derisively labeled the alt-lite by the true believers in the alt-right, railed against the political violence of the Left, obliquely lending its support to the embattled president they revered. The two groups, in fact, hated each other—evidence, perhaps, that the far right was already splintering. But they also had common cause: both gatherings were billed as rallies for free speech, and both saw freedom of speech as license to say any damned thing they wanted. The time-honored notions that one person's free speech ends where another's safety and freedom begins, that shouting "fire" in a crowded movie theater is not, in fact, protected speech, had been discarded without thought.

At the Lincoln Memorial, Matthew Lyons, a self-described

"scientific illuminist," warned against the parasites clinging to the white race. "You can leave them be; they die and the organism dies with them, or kill them and save the organism."

Another fixture of the new white nationalist movement, Michael Peinovich, also known as "Mike Enoch," cut to the chase: "Instead of giving another paean to free speech, yeah, yeah, great, we all love it, I'm actually gonna fucking use it. . . . The real battle is fought on the grounds of standing up for white people," he bellowed into the microphone before dishing out the red meat to the faithful. He rattled through the endless signs of the coming "white genocide," the diversity imperative that is depriving whites of jobs and admissions to higher education, the hordes of brown and black people fleeing terrible lands to sully ours without invitation from the upstanding white people. "Tell me what fucking rule we broke? Sorry for winning," he shouted to cheers. Oddly, a man stood next to him with a sign that read "Jews for Trump" in English and Hebrew. But that didn't stop Enoch from launching a call-and-response on who controls the media, who controls the Federal Reserve, who controls Hollywood, who controls Wall Street: the Jews, the Jews, the Jews.

"You will not replace us! You will not replace us! You will not replace us!" the crowd at the Lincoln Memorial chanted.

There it was, a new movement of prejudice and hate largely born in the invisible fever swamp of the Internet, now present in the flesh and claiming a new battleground for the Age of Trump: speech itself.

As the rally wrapped up, its ostensible leader and keynote

speaker, Richard B. Spencer, the man credited with coining the phrase "alt-right," told the dispersing crowd, "Remember everyone, see you in Charlottesville." Clearly, this gathering was a dry run for bigger things.

As a child, I didn't take hate all that seriously, even though I grew up in the South, where racism remained casual and African American women came to my segregated neighborhood in north Atlanta in the morning, then went home in the evening, exhausted, on what we called the "maids bus." My family attended the most liberal Reform synagogue in the city, perhaps in the entire New South—the Hebrew Benevolent Congregation, known by everyone simply as "the Temple." It had a storied history in the civil rights movement and an ongoing relationship with the Ebenezer Baptist Church, where the Reverend Dr. King had once preached. But what I remember of my religious education was a near-constant lesson in Holocaust studies with a side of Zionism—the study of a past atrocity and a distant land, neither of which had much meaning to me. At one point in Sunday school, a friend and I put on a puppet show set in Auschwitz, where we joked about the gross and stinky latrines. Hate broadly, and anti-Semitism more narrowly, were that abstract and meaningless. We found it riotous.

And then, suddenly, it was neither abstract nor meaningless. The campaign of 2016 was well under way on May 18 of that year. Donald Trump had not yet won the Republican nomination for president, but he had marauded through most of the primary season by then, crushing Jeb Bush out of the gate, rendering Chris Christie a vassal, making mincemeat of Little Marco Rubio in his home state of Florida, and finally vanquishing Ted Cruz at his Waterloo, the Indiana primary, after mocking the appearance of his last rival's wife and accusing his father of helping to assassinate John F. Kennedy. Much of the cognoscenti still labored under some vague notion that Trump—not really a conservative, certainly not a liberal—would be stopped at the convention in July, although the mechanics of that engineered coup remained a mystery. He certainly would not be elected president. Meanwhile, pro-Trump and anti-Trump forces were clashing with bloody intensity in San Jose, California, and on the streets of Chicago. Lusty chants of "Lock her up!" rang out at all of the Republican candidate's rallies. Anti-Trump protesters—often black or Latino—were routinely pushed, punched, and kicked, with the politician at the podium growling his approval. Freedom of speech was no longer an inalienable right guaranteed by the Constitution but a concept to be fought over, defined, and redefined, and possessed by either the Right or the Left.

It was a watershed moment in American culture. We just didn't realize it.

Like many journalists, I was active on Twitter and Facebook, using social media to promote my thoughts and writing, to share pieces that my friends and colleagues wrote, and to engage an audience that I hoped would read my articles in the *New York Times*. Politicians used social media as well, but usually in the dullest way, to broadcast pabulum ("On this Father's Day, let us all honor our fathers"), promote meaningless slogans ("A Better Way"), or share partisan talking points generated by their leadership or consultants ("Obamacare is imploding"; "The rich need to pay their fair share"). Then there was Donald Trump who, long before his maiden run for office, had used Twitter as a window into his id, a mechanism to blurt out his ugliest thoughts and direct his army of followers. Few of us yet understood the power of that tool and what it could unleash.

On that May morning, the *Washington Post* published a column by Robert Kagan, a Jewish neoconservative at the Brookings Institution known in Washington for backing the invasion of Iraq but little known outside of Washington. The piece was on the rise of fascism in the United States.

I liked its step-by-step breakdown of how authoritarianism could rise in the world's greatest democracy. Kagan wrote of the stark choice that political figures face with the rise of the autocratic strongman: "Get right with the leader and his mass following or get run over." Ambition may lead a politician onto the fascist bandwagon. No matter how incoherent the Dear Leader's speech, the ambitious pol praises his wisdom in hope of "a plum post in the new order," Kagan wrote. Others just hope to survive. They mumble their pledges of support and pray for the best. Others will put their heads down, believing the storm will pass and they will pick up the pieces, rebuild, and get back to normal. "Meanwhile, don't alienate the leader's mass following. After all, they are voters and will need to be brought back into the fold. As for Trump himself, let's shape him, advise him, steer him in the right direction and, not incidentally, save our political skins."

As I often do, I grabbed a snippet of a quote and released it to Twitter. I have a lot of followers—not celebrity level, not even a huge number for a Washington journalist, but in the tens of thousands. I don't say that to brag. Boasting about the number of your Twitter followers is like boasting about the number of kids who want to sit at your table in the middle school cafeteria. It's just not that revelatory.

Within minutes, I received a response with punctuation I had never seen before.

"Hello (((Weisman)))," wrote "CyberTrump."

Nothing more. Just that. I was sitting at my desk at work. I had some time on my hands as an editor at the *Times*, since my responsibilities then centered on domestic policy—economics, the environment, poverty—and with the nation consumed in this strange presidential campaign, not a lot of policy making was going on.

"Care to explain?" I answered, intuiting that my last name in those triple parentheses must somehow denote my Jewish faith.

"What, ho, the vaunted Ashkenazi intelligence, hahaha!" "CyberTrump" came back. "It's a dog whistle, fool. Belling the cat for my fellow goyim." With the cat belled, the horde followed.

What I didn't know was that I had unwittingly exposed what was known in the alt-right as "echoes," those three parentheses that practitioners of online harassment wrapped around Jewish-sounding names on social media. Unbeknown to, well, just about everyone, alt-right anti-Semites had created a Google plug-in that could be used to search double or triple parentheses, since ordinary search engines do not pick up punctuation marks. Haters would slap these "echoes" around Jewish-sounding names of people online they wanted to target. Once a target was "belled," the alt-right anti-Semitic mob could download the innocuous-sounding Coincidence Detector plug-in from the Google Chrome store, track down targets like heat-seeking missiles, then swarm.

"You've all provoked us. You've been doing it for decades—and centuries even—and we've finally had enough," declared Andrew Anglin, the creator and mastermind of the neo-Nazi website the Daily Stormer. "Challenge has been accepted."

And swarm they did.

"Trump God Emperor" sent me the Nazi iconography of the shiftless, hook-nosed Jew. I was served an image of the gates of Auschwitz, the famous words *Arbeit macht frei* replaced without irony with "Machen Amerika Great." Holocaust taunts, like a path of dollar bills leading into an oven, were followed by Holocaust denial—a classic trope of modern-day anti-Semitism: *The Holocaust didn't happen, but boy, was it cool.* The Jew as leftist puppet master from "DonaldTrumpLA"—an image of a giant, bulbous-nosed, shifty puppeteer holding the strings of equally offensive caricatures of feminists, Black Lives Matter activists, Occupy Wall Street types, and the like—was joined by other tropes: the Jew as conservative fifth columnist, the Jew as moneybags financier orchestrating war for Israel, the Jew as leftist anarchist, the Jew as rapacious, the Jew as Wall Street profiteer, the Jew as weak and sniveling, the Jew as all-powerful.

It popped up on my computer while I edited stories or chatted with reporters. It pinged on my iPhone in the Metro or while I was driving. For weeks, more than a thousand—maybe more than two thousand—such messages flooded my electronic life, usually as Twitter notifications but also as emails and voice mails. I hadn't known that virulent anti-Semitism still existed in America; now, I couldn't avoid it. The Jew can be all things to some people, it seems, none of them good.

"It is now fully documented that Jews are behind mass-immigration, feminism, the news media and Hollywood, pornography, the global banking system, global communism, the homosexual political agenda, the wars in the Middle East and virtually everything else the Alt-Right is opposed to," Anglin wrote on his Daily Stormer website in an extensive guide to the alt-right, the burgeoning new white nationalist movement that I had tapped into. "This is, to a shocking extent, simply admitted by the Jews themselves."

Anglin's sentiments are old, even ancient. But Anglin is not. He is a figure of our time, one of the men—I have come across no such women—who ushered old-line anti-Semitism into the Internet era with his Daily Stormer, which was the most heavily trafficked neo-Nazi website in the world until GoDaddy and Google refused to host it in August 2017, citing incitement to violence as violating their terms of service. The move temporarily pushed the Daily Stormer onto the "dark web," accessible only with special browsers that conceal the user's identity and location. It has popped up again under obscure but accessible Internet addresses only to be chased back into the sewer like an unwanted rat. The site has extolled the heroism of Anders Breivik, the Norwegian terrorist who murdered seventy-seven people—mostly children—in 2011, and whose readers included Dylann Roof, who gunned down African American parishioners after they invited him to join their Bible study group in the basement of Mother Emanuel AME Church in Charleston. Anglin has a way with words and an appreciation for how social media, email, and the good old telephone can be harnessed by an army of online "trolls" to torture an identified target. He has hackers at his beck and call to find and publish addresses, phone numbers, Social Security numbers, and other identifying information—an act known as "doxing." And he has minions to make the release of that information sting.

The imaginings by my tormentors of me as an Orthodox Jew in wide-brimmed hat and Hasidic garb were, of course, laughable. I shop, when I shop, at Banana Republic or J.Crew or, if feeling pinched, at Marshalls, like everyone else. I worry about my weight and try to make time for the gym. I'm not much into davening or prayer of a less expressive sort, either. My invocations of God come all too often in profane moments of surprise or anger. Long black coats always struck me as heavy, hot, and unflattering.

For an assimilated Jew, that moment—the "Who, me? Why me?" shock—is indelible. We live lives of unstudied ordinariness, not particularly proud or aware of our assimilation, unconscious of the conformity that has meshed us with American society over the decades. Jews don't live in ghettos anymore; most don't live in particularly Jewish neighborhoods. When we stand out, we do so in the same way the rest of America does: through achievement or failure, purple hair or studied fashionableness, inherited and cultivated good looks or physical disability. Then, in this odd moment, we are singled out for the one trait we have stopped thinking much about: being Jewish. How did anyone even notice me? I thought, perplexed as much as anguished.

The truth is, I had become largely disconnected from Jewish

life and faith, and like many American Jews I had been lulled into complacency. I was bar mitzvahed, sure, but that was a long time ago, with minimal effort and as little Hebrew as I could get away with. A professional choir (drawn in large part from the Peachtree Christian Church across the street) sang behind the curtains of my synagogue. I bought a Fender Telecaster with the proceeds. I still have it, though my high school girlfriend—Baptist, of course—seems to have kept my Peavey amplifier.

My Jewish identity in college and during my young adult life was observed mainly in the breach, through a brief infatuation with the Palestinian cause that brought me to an Arab village in northern Israel and an international peace commune in East Jerusalem; through my marriage to the towheaded daughter of a Pentecostalist from Appleton, Wisconsin; to the birth of my two daughters, whose gender absolved me of the potentially difficult choice of whether to have a bris.

As my infant daughters grew into childhood, Judaism became my guilty conscience, the thing I wanted for them but could not attain from my wife, who reasoned, logically, that raising the children Jewish would leave her an outsider in her own family. She had no interest in converting and had no expectation that I would accept Jesus as my savior. Best to slip to the lowest common denominator—nothing.

I would drag Hannah and Alissa to the free High Holy Day services at a local university, joining the other misfits from mixed marriages or tentative religious affiliations, smiling awkwardly, children in tow: islands of misfit Jews that formed for two weeks in the fall, dispersed like that mythical trash flow somewhere in the Pacific, then re-formed a year later. The girls hated it. They spoke no Hebrew, recognized no friends in the crowd, and had little context for that annual exposure to an ancient religion other than the springtime trek to Atlanta for Passover with Grandma (from the assimilated Upper West Side of Manhattan side of the family) and Zayde (from the identified Jewish Queens side of the family).

I would make my way through the season of Jewish guilt every fall, then assume my defensive crouch as the season of the Christmas tree, pine wreaths, nutcrackers, faux holly, plastic berries, and garish-but-temporary objets d'holiday approached, bearing the next wave of guilt—the sins of Jewish omission giving way to the sins of intermarriage commission.

But to say that my life in assimilated America was all disorientation and depression would be to severely overstate my dysphoria. Until the rise of Trumpism, Judaism was easy, not just for me but for millions of American Jews. It was cafeteria-style: observe or don't, join a synagogue or attend the occasional Jewish film festival, read Philip Roth, eat bagels and babka, say "oy" ironically. You could be Jewish by religion, Jewish by culture, Jewish by birth or identity—take your pick. In October 2013, the Pew Research Center asked the American Jewish community what it meant to be Jewish. The answers said a lot: 73 percent, the largest category, said remembering the Holocaust, followed by another category that was even more nebulous, who said leading a moral or ethical life. Then there were the 56 percent who said that being a Jew meant working for justice and equality, the 49 percent who said it meant being intellectually curious, the 43 percent who said it meant caring about Israel, separated by a statistically insignificant gap from the 42 percent who said it meant having a good sense of humor. Second from the bottom, at 19 percent, was observing Jewish law, followed only by eating traditional Jewish food.

Oy.

Our politics, once almost wholly liberal and Democratic, are now dispersed between the parties. As Republicans and Democrats fought over which party was more pro-Israel, which party was more open to Judeo-Christian ideals, which party was more open to Jewish voters (and donors), Jews felt their place in society comfortably cushioned in bipartisanship. Our coreligionists graced our movie screens (Natalie Portman! Scarlett Johansson! Winona Ryder!) and led the cities of Los Angeles and Chicago (Rahm! He was on a first-name basis with all of us, regardless of whether we loved him or thought him a schmuck). We succeeded without apology but also struggled like everyone else. Anti-Semitism was in the past. The "Jewish Question" was little worth mentioning.

And then, all at once, it was. On my phone, on my computer, in my voice mail. The information technology guys in my office asked if I had called the police (I hadn't). I got that sad cancer face from colleagues and friends—I'm so sorry about what you're going through. Strangers on the Internet told their followers and friends, if you want to see how ugly things are getting, check out @jonathanweisman's Twitter mentions. I brushed it aside, but I couldn't stop looking. Like the tongue finds the tooth with the ache, my eyes were drawn to my correspondents.

"I found the Menorah you were looking for," one of them offered with a Trump-triumphant backdrop on his Twitter profile; it was a candelabrum made of the number 6 million— *Didn't happen, but man, was it cool.* "Old Grand Dad" cheerfully sent over a patriotic image of Donald Trump in colonial garb holding up the Liberty Bell and fighting "against the foreign hordes" with caricatures of the Jew, the American Indian, the Mexican, the Chinese, and the Irish cowering at his feet.

I was certainly not the only Jewish journalist to experience the onslaught. Julia Ioffe is a gifted freelance journalist who covered the 2016 campaign (she now writes for *The Atlantic*). She was born in Moscow but driven out of the Soviet Union during in its last dying days in the 1980s by resurgent anti-Semitism. In April she wrote a profile of Melania Trump for *GQ* magazine that revealed that Melania had a half-brother with whom her family was not in contact. Hardly Watergate, but the revelation did not sit well with the future first lady or her husband. "My parents are private citizens and should not be subject to Ms. Ioffe's unfair scrutiny," Melania Trump wrote on Facebook on April 24. For the Trumps' army of anti-Semites, she might as well have written, "Will no one rid me of this troublesome priest?" Ioffe was served up on social media in concentration camp garb, threatened with rape, pictured kneeling, hands bound, brains being blown out by a Nazi executioner.

"I don't control my fans," Melania told an interviewer, waving off Ioffe's treatment with a faint *pshaw*. "She provoked them."

Bethany Mandel is a young, Orthodox, stay-at-home mom in New Jersey who writes for the *Forward*, an influential Jewish news outlet, as a conservative, often on social issues such as abortion. A social conservative with a buoyant, smiling face and a penchant for bragging about her children, she is hardly the profile of a target of right-wing hate, certainly not the "social justice warrior" the trolls love to loathe. But an off-handed anti-Trump tweet after the South Carolina primary drew scrutiny from Trump supporters, who, shall we say, did not bother to read her other work. She was called a "slimy Jewess," threatened with sexual assault, and told she "deserved the oven." One anonymous tormenter electronically harassed her for nineteen hours straight. When she received death threats in her private Facebook mailbox, she filed a police report—then bought a gun.

She had company in the growing camp of armed Jewry.

"I have augmented my firearms collection and training, obtained a Concealed Carry weapon permit, and became a NRA life member because of the approval of violence Trump has encouraged," Nathan Wurtzel, a Republican strategist, told her, a quote she included in her *Forward* column in March 2016, not long before I felt the same lash. "It's not just the anti-Semitism of his most ardent fans, but the general breakdown of civil society they seek. I think all American Jews should be armed per the laws of their state."

Hadas Gold—Tel Aviv born, Arizona raised, and editor of Politico's *On the Media* blog—appears to have done nothing more offensive than write about the presidential campaign with a Jewish name. For her sins, she was presented online with a Nazi-era yellow *Jude* star affixed to her chest and the warning, "Aliyah or line up by the wall, your choice." (*Aliyah* is the term for Jews emigrating to Israel.) "What does it say about this election that I'm so meh about really crazy anti-Semitic attacks on me on social media and via email?" she asked on Twitter on October 16.

For women Jewish journalists, the anti-Semitic threat was mixed with an ominous menace of sexual violence.

The Anti-Defamation League tasked a group of venerable journalists, led by Steve Coll, the former managing editor of the *Washington Post*, to catalogue the attacks. Their findings: 2.6 million anti-Semitic messages posted on Twitter from August 2015 to July 2016, of which 19,253 were directed at journalists. The onslaught climbed significantly as the presidential race heated up. More than 800 journalists were subjected to anti-Semitic attacks on Twitter, but ten of them received 83 percent of the total attacks. I was number five on that Top Ten list.

Beyond the Internet and beyond journalism, the pace of

the assaults on multiethnic, multicultural democracy was only picking up steam. It would be foolish to think that hate this virulent would confine itself to commentary. It was certainly not confined to Jews. Muslims have been physically assaulted by Trump supporters. An Indian engineer in Kansas was gunned down by a man shouting, "Get out of my country!" His widow was later targeted for deportation. Hispanics—many of them not immigrants—have been taunted and threatened. Undocumented immigrants are being hauled from their homes, schools, and workplaces for deportation. Groups that had been maligned over centuries at different times in different regions now shared a common tormentor: the alt-right, a militant agglomeration of white nationalists, racists, anti-Semites, and America Firsters that had been waging war on the Republican establishment for some time.

Richard Bertrand Spencer, one of the leaders of this new white nationalist movement, had been bouncing around racist, anti-Semitic circles through the Obama years. A son of privilege, born in Boston to an ophthalmologist and a cotton heiress, Spencer graduated from St. Mark's School of Texas, the kind of broad-lawned private school where the boys wear white blazers to commencement, attend chapel, and have access to a planetarium. He majored in English and music at the University of Virginia, earned a master's in the humanities from the University of Chicago, and studied in Vienna for two summers. His unfinished doctoral work at Duke was in modern European intellectual history. In short, he seemed as if he had nothing much to be angry about. Spencer burst into the public consciousness during the Trump campaign. His stiff-armed "Hail Trump" salute in full view of television cameras and print reporters on the eve of Trump's inauguration made him something of a household antihero. He was famously sucker-punched in the face while doing an interview on Trump's inauguration day. The video of this sparked both cheers and hand-wringing from liberals uncertain about the aptness of cheering violence.

The alt-right's court jester, Milo Yiannopoulos, had also lived largely on the fringes, a silver-tongued provocateur at Breitbart, the conservative news website run by Trump campaign chief Steve Bannon and unofficial organ of the alt-right. He spoke with a posh English accent, specialized in taunting the Left, reveled in mocking women, and was an expert at seeking publicity. Then Trump was elected, and Yiannopoulos was invited to speak at the 2017 Conservative Political Action Conference, the circus-like gabfest of the American Conservative Union. He had arrived. The ACU was once a staid guardian of traditional conservatism, standing athwart history and shouting "No"—William F. Buckley types with pipes and principles: small government, low taxes, but also tolerance. With the Yiannopoulos invitation and the slavish devotion to all things Trump, the organization that invented conservative ratings for lawmakers now believes hate is worthy of engagement. Images of Yiannopoulos posing with a stack of Hitler biographies and cradling a Nazi-era iron cross didn't get him disinvited, nor did the stream of invective about "whinging Black Lives Matter activists," "whining feminists," and Jews that run, well, everything. The line was crossed when videotape surfaced of him extolling the virtues of homosexual relationships between older men and boys as young as thirteen. It is good to know that while anti-Semitism and racism are tolerable points of debate for the American Conservative Union, pedophilia and statutory rape are still beyond the pale. We all have our limits.

But fear not. As a consolation, Milo's benefactors quickly raised $12 million to finance MILO, Inc., a touring company of alt-right provocateurs dedicated to "making the lives of journalists, professors, politicians, feminists, Black Lives Matter activists and other professional victims a living hell." After Yiannopoulos's book contract was canceled, he self-published his memoir, *Dangerous*, and launched it with a Manhattan book party that featured strippers who began their tease in full-length burkas, dancing dwarves in yarmulkes, and Milo himself snapping the necks of left-wing impersonators.

"Free speech is back—and it is fabulous," he declared in his launch statement.

Then came Charlottesville and the "Unite the Right" rally that seemed to change everything—or at least forced a sleeping nation to confront its new reality. A racist, anti-Semitic mob gathered with its Nazi flags and "Jews are Satan's children" placards not far from the green of the University of Virginia, founded by the man who wrote that we are all endowed with certain unalienable rights. Tiki torches and chants of "Jews will not replace us!" provided the indelible images and sounds of the summer of 2017. Then an Ohio man named James Alex Fields Jr., who had marched earlier sporting the white polo shirt and black shield of Vanguard America, a group dedicated to white supremacy and fighting the international Jew, sped his Dodge Challenger into a crowd of counterdemonstrators gathered to celebrate the dispersal of the hate-mongers. Heather Heyer, a young Charlottesville paralegal, died; dozens were injured; and the notions of peaceful assembly and free speech were stripped bare.

The nation gasped.

There are broader crosscurrents in all this. The Right has successfully seized the cause of free speech in recent years, defining tolerance as the mandatory acceptance of intolerance. The alt-right popularized the term "special snowflake" for those delicate-hearted liberals who can't quite stomach bigoted provocation, and the term now has wide currency on the nation's campuses, where the battle lines are most clearly drawn. A sitting member of Congress, Steve King of Iowa, can declare, "I'd like to see an America that's so homogeneous that we look a lot the same," and we are supposed to accept this in the name of free expression. Kim Weaver, King's would-be Democratic opponent in the 2018 midterm elections, dropped out of the race the summer before, citing on her Facebook page as one of the reasons "alarming acts of intimidation, including death threats." A Republican state representative from Mississippi, whose district includes the site where fourteen-year-old Emmett Till was beaten, mutilated, shot, and thrown into the waters of the Tallahatchie River, says any leader who allows Confederate memorials to be taken down "should be LYNCHED." We *tsk tsk*. The far left has responded with ever more dramatic displays of militant policing of speech. A shout-down of the conservative scholar Charles Murray at Middlebury College sparked Milo Yiannopoulos to wade onto the campus of the University of California at Berkeley, a provocation that was greeted with just the anarchist melee that he was hoping for. Not content with one violent clash between right-wing thugs and left-wing anarchists, verbal bomb thrower Ann Coulter decided that she, too, would speak at Berkeley, only to back down in the face of militant special snowflakery.

After the tragic shooting of Republican Representative Steve Scalise on a baseball practice field in the summer of 2017, a new cry arose from the alt-right. The shooter, who was killed by the police, was an unhinged leftist, a follower of Bernie Sanders who hated Trump. In his actions and death, the far right found a side cause to their free speech movement: standing up to the violence of the Left. Their victimhood neared completion; their own predations took another step toward carte blanche. Even after the bloody showdown in Charlottesville, alt-right defiance took the form of victimhood. It was the anti-fascist, or Antifa, movement that did it; it was the police that allowed it; it was the white man, again, who was oppressed. Even President Trump's oh-so-mild displays of moral umbrage were greeted by the white supremacists with shouts of outrage.

"So, after decades of White Americans being targeted for discriminated [*sic*] & anti-White hatred, we come together as a people, and you attack us?" demanded David Duke, the former Klan leader and unrepentant white supremacist, on Twitter in August 2017.

Through all this we are becoming unmoored from an agreed-upon reality. Our president can accuse our former president of wiretapping him, then send his consigliere, Kellyanne Conway, out to the cameras to declare, "I'm not Inspector Gadget. . . . I'm not in the job of having evidence. That's what investigations are for." His near-daily attacks on the "Fake Media," the "Failing New York Times," "Dumb as a Rock Mika Brzezinski," "Crazy Joe Scarborough," and "Fraudulent CNN" are meant to disorient us, to make us question truth itself, or, short of that, at least to inure his followers from the influence of actual events and an accumulation of data points that might shake their faith in him. The television journalist Megyn Kelly invited right-wing conspiracy theorist Alex Jones to be interviewed on her prime-time NBC news show to discuss his contemptible assertion that the massacre of twenty children at Sandy Hook Elementary School was a "false flag" production of the Obama administration to push gun control; then, amid the outcry, she asked the parents of murdered children to appear on the show to defend the objective reality of their grief. They declined.

And we seem to be paralyzed in the face of the far right's forcible seizure of the free speech movement. It's hostage taking. A few weeks before the Southern Baptist Convention's annual meeting in the summer of 2017, an African American minister from Texas, Dwight McKissic, published on a blog a draft resolution audaciously proclaiming that "there has arisen in the United States a growing menace to political order and justice that seeks to reignite social animosities, reverse improvements in race relations, divide our people, and foment hatred, classism, and ethnic cleansing," naming this "toxic menace" as white nationalism and the alt-right.

His draft resolution called on the convention to "reject the retrograde ideologies, xenophobic biases, and racial bigotries of the so-called 'Alt-Right' that seek to subvert our government, destabilize society, and infect our political system."

The result wasn't a unanimous vote of steadfast courage. It was chaos. The convention dithered, worried sick about the 81 percent of Evangelicals who voted for Trump. Divisions that lay beneath the surface of the Southern Baptist world burst into the open: divisions over race, politics, and hate. What was missing from the debate was religion and faith. A religious order could not take a firm stand against hate. "We were very aware that on this issue, feelings rightly run high regarding alt-right ideology," Barrett Duke, the head of the resolutions committee, told a reporter for the *Atlantic*. "We share those feelings. . . . We just weren't certain we could craft a resolution that would enable us to measure our strong convictions with the grace of love, which we're also commended by Jesus to incorporate."

What Would Jesus Do? Equivocate, I guess.

Unsurprisingly, black ministers were furious. "We must be clear: We live in a time when equivocating on these matters furthers the sin of racism even to violence and death," wrote Thabiti Anyabwile, a black Southern Baptist pastor, in a tweet. "Any 'church' that cannot denounce white supremacy without hesitancy and equivocation is a dead, Jesus denying assembly. No 2 ways about it."

Richard Spencer was exultant amid the turmoil, which was reported from Phoenix by a blogger and freelance journalist, Sarah Posner. Presumably, it was her last name that elicited this comment on Twitter: "The irony of jews who imagine themselves to be morally superior accusing whites of supremacism." The Jew is the oppressor; the white man is the victim.

A week and a half before Election Day, I spoke to a group composed largely of elderly Jews in a community center just beyond the D.C. line in Maryland—one of those small, nebulous villages—this one called Friendship Heights—that really has no right to be autonomous of the metropolis around it. "In ten days," I said, "the United States will have elected its first woman president. The question at that moment will be whether the hate and division that surfaced during the 2016 campaign will be remembered as a last gasp of a defeated populace, clinging desperately to the old order they once ruled as it was swept away, or the beginning of a recalcitrant movement against American democratic pluralism." Most members of the audience applauded with the same smug certainty that I was showing.

One man, though, with a strong Central European accent, stooped over a cane, spoke to me afterward. "I have seen movements like this before," he told me. "They are not so easily dismissed."

Like so many other members of the Washington cognoscenti, I had been dead wrong. I could justify it. Oh, Hillary Clinton won the popular vote by nearly 3 million; her 2 percent win was the largest of any losing presidential candidate since the disputed election of 1876. Had it not been for the Russians, or James Comey, or Anthony Weiner, or Jill Stein, surely she would have won Wisconsin, Michigan, and Pennsylvania, which she lost collectively by a smaller number than a capacity crowd at Lambeau Field. Perhaps all true, but I was wrong nonetheless.

And since that miscalculation, the troubles have grown for Jews, leaping from the abstraction of the Internet to the reality of toppled headstones at Jewish cemeteries in St. Louis and Philadelphia, swastikas as graffiti, and bomb threats against synagogues and Jewish community centers, daycare facilities, and schools.

As with all sensitive matters in our sprawling, polyglot country, the new anti-Semitism is complicated. At a private meeting with state attorneys general, President Trump was asked about the rise of anti-Semitic threats. He told the attorney general of Pennsylvania, Josh Shapiro (who is Jewish), "You've got to be careful. It could be the reverse. This could be the reverse, trying to make people look bad."

That "false flag" accusation was greeted with a new round of outrage by some Jewish groups and liberals, although, as with so many outrageous statements from the president, most stayed silent. Always best to wait and see. And perhaps they were proven right. When the first arrest was made in the bomb threats, the alleged perpetrator was a black former journalist of questionable mental health. He had apparently been phoning in the threats to get back at an ex-girlfriend. The coup de grâce came when a Jewish American-Israeli teenager was arrested in Israel, allegedly for having phoned in the lion's share of the threats. Conservatives immediately hailed the genius of Trump's warning and demanded an apology from all those who had claimed that his nationalism, reluctance to speak out, or sins of omission had fostered the attacks. David Duke's white supremacist website declared that the arrest was made only after Trump sent a "trusted team of FBI agents to Israel to get to the bottom of this matter." That gave Duke and his sidekick from Andrew Anglin's neo-Nazi Daily Stormer website, Eric Striker (who called himself "the winner of 'the Daily Stormer Was Right and the Jews Lied' award"), a chance to launch into a lengthy diatribe on the history of Jewish psychological warfare efforts against innocent white folks.

Yes, it's complicated; but perhaps the reason mentally unstable young men were phoning in bomb threats to Jewish schools, community centers, and daycare centers was because anti-Semitism was in the news and in the national bloodstream. It would resonate.

"We have to ask ourselves, are people emboldened by the inflammatory rhetoric around them?" James Comey, the director of the FBI, asked a lunch crowd at a conference of the Anti-Defamation League in May 2017 in Washington. He didn't answer. He didn't need to. Donald Trump fired him a few days later.

Well after the arrests of those two bomb-threat callers, supporters of the president held a rally in Huntington Beach, California, one of several small but spirited pro-Trump gatherings that day. On the sands of Orange County, one Trump supporter held aloft a sign that read simply "Da Goyim Know." It is a popular anti-Semitic meme from the Internet, code to the alt-right world, short for "Da Goyim Know, Shut It Down," as in *Oh, no! The non-Jews have discovered our nefarious plot to control the world! Better close down the operation.* "Da Goyim Know"—the alt-right has your number, Jew. No, it doesn't make sense to us, but it does to the initiated, and it had jumped from the virtual world to the very real one as punches flew between protesters and counterprotesters. There was nothing intangible or high-tech about fists connecting to faces on that beach.

"Nothing scares the destroyers of Western Civilization more than this: 'Da Goyim Know.' We are reaching critical mass and they know it," David Duke crowed in a March 26, 2017, tweet, signing off, "Make America Great Again."

In Charlottesville, before blood started flowing in the streets, Duke told the media crowded around him, "We are going to fulfill the promises of Donald Trump. That's what we believed in. That's why we voted for Donald Trump."

Whether he knew it or not, Donald Trump ran the most anti-Semitic presidential campaign in modern American history. At this time, in November of 2017, I still maintain that he didn't know it. But haplessness is not a defense. When grainy visages of Goldman Sachs chairman Lloyd Blankfein and Federal Reserve chairwoman Janet Yellen grace the television screen on your closing campaign ad as the narrator darkly denounces the "global special interests," someone on Trump's campaign knew. His audience in the alt-right certainly knew. At one point, after Trump retweeted a put-down of Jeb Bush by "WhiteGenocideTM," the neo-Nazi who had previously professed his admiration for Hitler, another white nationalist, "TheNordicNation," approvingly proclaimed, "You can say #WhiteGenocide now, Trump has brought it into the mainstream"—white genocide being the risible notion that the increasing power of Jews, African Americans, Latinos, and other minorities, not to mention the mingling of racial blood, constitutes a planned threat to the Caucasian race.

When Donald Trump was finally asked to his face about the rise of anti-Semitism, he launched into an incoherent screed on his political strength among some unspecified groups that hadn't liked Republicans in the past, his Jewish daughter, and his Electoral College margin. The questioner, Jake Turx, a Hasidic journalist with *Ami Magazine*, picked by Trump as a friendly face, didn't disappoint. Clearly, he had not intended to offend the president.

"Despite what some of my colleagues may have been reporting, I haven't seen anybody in my community accuse either yourself or anyone on your staff of being anti-Semitic. We understand that you have Jewish grandchildren. You are their *zayde*," Turx said gently, his skull cap on, his *payot* tucked behind his ears.

Trump nodded slightly and murmured, "Thank you."

"However, what we are concerned about, and what we haven't really heard being addressed, is an uptick in anti-Semitism and how the government is planning to take care of it. There's been a report out that forty-eight bomb threats have been made against Jewish centers all across the country in the last couple of weeks. There are people committing anti-Semitic acts and threatening to—"

For the president of the United States, that was enough.

"Sit down," he commanded. "I understand the rest of your question."

He then assured us all that he was "the least anti-Semitic person you've ever seen in your life."

"I hate the charge. I find it repulsive," he sputtered as he shouted down the sympathetic reporter in the White House's ornate East Room. "I hate even the question because people that know me . . ." And with that, his verbiage spun into nonsense. He never answered the question: When are you going to address the uptick in anti-Semitism?

By now, we are all wondering if it was the right question. Anti-Semitism is a pestilence that has survived millennia, raging at some times, retreating at other times into carriers that have passed it on in silence through the generations. The questions, then, are what triggered its latest outbreak, how were we again caught unawares, and what are we going to do about it?

ONE

Complacency

The Jew flourishes when borders come down, when boundaries blur, when walls are destroyed, not erected. Rabbi Moses ben Maimon—better known as Maimonides—was, to Western culture, perhaps the first Jewish citizen of the world, or at least of the Muslim world. There were others. Hasdai ibn Shaprut served functionally as the foreign minister of Abd al Rachman, the Moorish ruler of the Iberian Peninsula in the Middle Ages. Shmuel HaNagid was a powerful military leader under Muslim rule around the same time. But Maimonides lives on beyond the academy, a legend to this day. Born in Moorish Cordoba, Spain, on Passover eve, sometime around 1135, he was a rabbi, physician, scientist, and scholar, taking advantage of the relative tolerance of the Islamic empire to travel, learn, and teach. National borders and identity were in one of those cyclical ebbs as Maimonides journeyed from

Spain to Morocco, from Morocco to Egypt, from Egypt to the Holy Land of his people, then back to Egypt. His interpretations of Torah, his observations of asthma, diabetes, hepatitis, and pneumonia, his dismissals of astrology, his Thirteen Principles of Faith and observations of law spread from the Iberian Peninsula to the Jewish communities of Yemen and Iraq, through the written word and the caravansaries of the *ummah*, where national identity had dissolved under the influence of religion and boundaries were set by the soldiers of the faithful.

This is not to say that those pre-medieval years marked a halcyon moment of religious freedom and Jewish expression. There were forced conversions and spasms of violence. But long before the Enlightenment of the eighteenth century, the notion of the man of no nation had existed—to the benefit of the Jews of the Mediterranean diaspora.

It was not until the Enlightenment that the concept of the European really emerged, and that First European was Jewish. Well into the 1700s, many European cities denied residency to Jews or crowded them into ghettos. In 1752, the British Parliament approved a law allowing Jews to become naturalized citizens of the empire, but the public uproar was so great that the law was hurriedly repealed. But Jews clamored for freedom, a freedom disconnected from national boundaries and united by enlightened ideas of universal rights.

In southern France, an educated, affluent Jewish community emerged, its members accepted as part of the bourgeoisie.

In the German states, Moses Mendelssohn almost single-handedly reshaped the image of the Jew as a worldly, educated sophisticate who could capture the imagination of society, all the while clinging to his faith. Educated, affluent Jews were the intellectual shock troops of the Enlightenment.

The French Revolution and the Declaration of the Rights of Man included Jews of French heritage under the umbrella of their protection. In 1806, Napoleon convened the Grand Sanhedrin of European Jewry—a reconstituted high court of Jewish wise men—to answer his twelve questions:

1. Is it lawful for Jews to have more than one wife?
2. Is divorce allowed by the Jewish religion? Is divorce valid, although pronounced not by courts of justice but by virtue of laws in contradiction to the French code?
3. May a Jewess marry a Christian, or may a Jew marry a Christian woman? Or does Jewish law order that the Jews should only intermarry among themselves?
4. In the eyes of Jews are Frenchmen not of the Jewish religion considered as brethren or as strangers?
5. What conduct does Jewish law prescribe toward Frenchmen not of the Jewish religion?
6. Do the Jews born in France, and treated by the law as French citizens, acknowledge France as their country? Are they bound to defend it? Are they

bound to obey the laws and follow the directions of the civil code?

7. Who elects the rabbis?

8. What kind of police jurisdiction do the rabbis exercise over the Jews? What judicial power do they exercise over them?

9. Are the police jurisdiction of the rabbis and the forms of the election regulated by Jewish law, or are they only sanctioned by custom?

10. Are there professions from which the Jews are excluded by their law?

11. Does Jewish law forbid the Jews to take usury from their brethren?

12. Does it forbid, or does it allow, usury in dealings with strangers?

Condescending? Sure. But Napoleon was putting the Jewish Question to the Jews rather than relegating them to the ghetto. Napoleon was satisfied with the Sanhedrin's answers, which included compromises to what Jewish law would allow in a new Europe. The Jews, Napoleon was convinced, would not be so otherly after all. And as French forces swept eastward under the banner of *Liberté, égalité, fraternité*, he freed them from their ghettos and allowed them to own property, to worship freely, and to apply themselves to professions from which old laws had barred them. Historians still argue over Napoleon's intentions, over whether he truly sympathized with the

Jews of the east or merely sought to undermine the order of the nation-states he was conquering. And of course, those conquered states have no love lost for the little Frenchman. But again, the Jews were the beneficiaries of the falling borders—and the victims of their reinstatement. After he drove back Napoleon, Czar Alexander I denounced the liberation of Jews and demanded the return of Jewish control laws. In Austria, as the French tide receded, Metternich fretted that the Jews would forever take Napoleon to be their messiah. The Lutherans of Prussia moved quickly to reverse Jewish liberation. And the triumphant Brits, the heroes of Waterloo, rejected the peace of the Sanhedrin.

But freedom is not easily rebottled. In 1867, as the borders of the Austro-Hungarian Empire expanded and the very notion of "nation" in Central Europe blurred, Emperor Franz Josef I formally conferred full and equal rights to the empire's Jews. A year later, Benjamin Disraeli—the man French philosopher Bernard-Henri Lévy calls "that supremely insolent Jew"—arose to become the prime minister of Pax Britannia, yet another global enterprise. Yes, technically he was a convert; but he was bold enough to declare that "little Jews" like him would carry "the spark of genius" to the British Isles—and to chastise fellow members of Parliament by saying that his ancestors "were in Jerusalem, priests in King Solomon's temple," while their kin, the Angles, Saxons, and Jutes, "were living in the forests of an unknown island."

Long before that, in 1654, the first boatload of Jews arrived in the New World, twenty-three Portuguese Jews from the Netherlands disembarking in what was then New Amsterdam. Peter Stuyvesant, the Dutch colonial governor, was none too pleased. Writing to the directors of the Dutch West Indies Company, he delicately advised, "We have, for the benefit of this weak and newly developing place and the land in general, deemed it useful to require them in a friendly way to depart, praying also most seriously in this connection, for ourselves as also for the general community of your worships, that the deceitful race—such hateful enemies and blasphemers of the name of Christ—be not allowed to further infect and trouble this new colony."

That didn't sit well with the few but powerful Jewish directors, who rejected his recommendation and ordered the refugees to stay. The Jews of America had a purchase.

Technically, the Jews of what became New York were not allowed to practice their religion freely, but by 1695 a map of the city publicly identified the synagogue on Beaver Street and noted the name of the rabbi, Saul Brown. In 1727, the General Assembly of New York declared that any British subject professing the Jewish faith need not utter the words "upon the true faith of a Christian" when taking a legal oath. That was twenty-five years before the Parliament in London tried and failed to allow Jews to become naturalized citizens of the empire. Jewish settlements were flourishing in Newport, Rhode Island; in Lancaster and Philadelphia, Pennsylvania; in Charleston, South Carolina; and in Savannah, Georgia. John Locke's charter for the Carolina Colonies granted "Jews, heathens, and dissenters" full liberty of conscience. Where national identity blurred, the Jew flourished. That was true even before the American officially existed in the Americas.

What became the United States would prove to be the stage for true Jewish liberation, after fits and starts, better times and worse.

Jonah Pesner, a rabbi and, since January 2015, president of Reform Judaism's Religious Action Center, a storied outpost in Washington that helped nurture the civil rights movement, tells the story of his grandmother, whom he remembers speaking in heavily accented English long after her arrival in America from Russia. Pesner is nearing fifty but looks much younger. His stories tell his age.

"I'd say, 'Are you Russian, grandma?' 'No,' she'd say, 'I'm Jewish.' 'But what do you mean? Why not Russian?' I'd press her on it. Finally, she'd say, 'Jonah, my father dug a hole underneath the floorboards so I could be hidden from the Cossacks coming to rape me. I saw the rabbi in my village tied by his beard to a cart and dragged from town. I am not Russian.'"

But we Jews in the United States are American; we value that identity—and most of us would like to keep it.

Contrary to the imaginings of the Twitter trolls, I'm a son of the South, not a Hasid from Crown Heights. (Perhaps the trolls didn't literally picture me this way; they were merely fond of

Photoshopping a black felt hat and *payot* on the pictures of me
that they could find through the magic of Google.) My father
grew up in Queens, New York. His mother was from Mon-
treal, where her father owned a shoe store. My father's father
was a doctor. His mother kept a kosher home, was a terrible
cook, and was fond of exclaiming, "I love being Jewish." They
lived in a modest house in Kew Gardens and made do. My
father battled bullies at school, at times enlisting his younger
but bigger brother Alan to do his fighting. My grandfather,
my Zayde, joined the Army during World War II, was shipped
off to Britain and a military hospital, and was in no rush to
come home after V-E Day. For a good chunk of his childhood, my dad, Evan Weisman, and his two brothers, Alan and
Hank, were raised by their mother, my Bubbe, alone.

My mother, Nancy Cowan Weisman, grew up on the Upper West Side of Manhattan, seemingly a million miles from
Queens. Her mother, a mostly assimilated Jew named Shirley
Cowan, ran a daycare center in Spanish Harlem and was not
so fond of saying she loved being Jewish. She would proclaim
that some of her best friends were Jewish. My mother had
a Christmas tree; trick-or-treated in the long hallways of the
Ansonia Hotel, where she grew up on the twelfth floor; and
went to Midnight Mass at St. Paul's because her parents liked
the music. She was the identified New Yorker.

My father was not. He went to medical school at Emory
University, in one of Atlanta's lovelier neighborhoods, where
wisteria vines grew wild and blossomed in great showy dis-

plays amid the thick Georgia tree cover. While he was in college, his parents decamped for Orlando, a nothing little town in Central Florida where a Seventh-day Adventist Hospital lured my Zayde after the war. It was then still mostly swamp, with no dreams of princess castles and human-size talking mice. My father had nothing left holding him to New York. He moved his family south in 1967—not to the quasi-South of Central Florida, but to Atlanta. I was two.

My parents joined a synagogue, not out of any sense of connection to Judaism but because my mother wanted to show her solidarity with Rabbi Jacob Rothschild, an outspoken leader of the civil rights movement whose activism had prompted the Ku Klux Klan to bomb the Temple. My Upper West Side mother wanted a piece of that action.

Being Jewish in Atlanta was not that unusual. Atlanta collected the oppressed of the Southeast—blacks, gays, Jews—a welcoming island in often hostile seas. Anti-Semitism existed in the casual "Jew me down" patois of the neighborhood kids. Once, on a school bus, I mentioned Camp Blue Star, a Jewish summer camp that some kids from my synagogue went to. "Jewish camp, is that like Auschwitz?" Will Buchanan asked. I laughed along with everyone else. I also remember my next-door neighbor, John Sisk, sheepishly telling me his mother had said something I wouldn't like. "What was it?" I asked suspiciously.

"She said you were a Jew."

"Yes, John, that's what we are called."

We both laughed.

The issue in 1970s Atlanta was racism, which was everywhere. The boys in my neighborhood—myself included—ran around after school in feral packs. We played a game in my best friend Frankie's yard that we told ourselves was some variant of rugby—basically, the kid with the football ran around and everyone else tried to tackle him. It was called "Kill the Nigger with the Ball," or sometimes "Smear the Queer." We also played sandlot football, and if someone shanked a punt, someone else invariably shouted, "Kick it like a white man!" Everyone—and I mean *everyone*—knew that the public transit system, MARTA, which brought the maids from the south side of town to the north, stood for Moving Africans Rapidly Through Atlanta. There was nothing subtle about race in the "City Too Busy To Hate," as our business leaders called it.

Outside Atlanta, things were far worse. As a young teenager in the late seventies, I went to a wilderness camp in the mountains of North Georgia run by the YMCA. It attracted black kids from downtown, the type of worldly, tough, inner-city teens who didn't mix with the suburban kids of Riverwood and North Springs high schools. When we were on-site at Camp Pioneer, in our bunks or in the mess hall, those kids introduced me to an urban life I didn't know existed: boasts of sex, lots of sex, at fourteen; casual chatter about weed and clubbing; and smack talk, even to the director of the camp. At the end of one session, each cabin of around ten teens made a commemorative plaque out of a slab of wood to recount all the adventures and good times that we would all miss. My cabin,

Comanche—six poor black kids on scholarship and four fairly affluent white kids, two of them Jewish, one of them gay— had spent weeks having run-ins with the camp authorities and coping with various punishments, such as KP duty and cleaning toilets. Once we had built a tower of dishes on our table that reached the ceiling. When it crashed to the ground there was hell to pay, even after Hawk, our ringleader, protested, "But we built a monument!" Hawk claimed he had taken the virginity of a white girl on the other side of camp, eliciting howls of delight from the other black guys in our cabin during a lengthy, extremely explicit kiss-and-tell session that had me convinced. The white kids were in awe. At the last campfire we presented our plaque, which read "Life's a Bitch and We Got the Switch." We etched it lovingly into a slab of wood, carved an electric switch, and signed our names. We were proud of it. The director threw it in the campfire. Off-site, on our way to a four-day backpacking trip on the Appalachian Trail, a five-day canoe trip on the Chattahoochee River, or an overnight rock-climbing excursion, it was another story. The same kids who had wowed me with their daring and audacity were petrified. They'd hide in the van when we stopped for gas and the locals peered in. "Yo, Jonathan, go in there and get us some MoonPies."

"Come in with me."

"You fuckin' kiddin' me? Imma mind my business right here. You see those crackers out there?"

It was a lesson in raw fear that I did not absorb until much,

much later. After Charlottesville and the hot summer of 2017, the Senate's only black Republican, Tim Scott of South Carolina, received an audience with President Trump at the White House to explain why he had said the president had lost his moral compass. Yes, the senator had explained, some of the counterdemonstrators who had confronted white supremacists in Charlottesville had been rowdy, even violent. They had squirted pepper spray and thrown punches. But the racists and anti-Semites carried with them a history of lynching, beating, rape, and murder that had left African Americans, especially in the South, terrorized, fearing for their lives and their children's lives. The specter of Klansmen in the open, of swastikas and Confederate flags in the public arena, had a power and resonance that no black-clad Antifa radical could carry. Real fear needed history. Tim Scott reminded me of my own childhood experiences. He seemed to have reminded Trump of nothing.

"He is who he has been, and I didn't go in there to change who he was," Senator Scott said after the meeting, a nonaudible sigh in his words. "I wanted to inform and educate a different perspective. I think we accomplished that and to assume that immediately thereafter he's going to have an epiphany is just unrealistic."

Anti-Semitism was different, a vague sense of the Other. Aside from my first two years in Salt Lake City, where my father was dodging the draft in the Public Health Service, I was an Atlantan. But my high school girlfriend's Southern

Baptist mother called me "the Yankee that Gage dates." I didn't catch the subtle anti-Semitic slight, and perhaps she didn't, either.

Anti-Semitism is like that, pressed underground by Jewish vigilance and ready umbrage. In 1994, when the conservative scholars Richard Herrnstein and Charles Murray published *The Bell Curve*, suggesting a genetic component to IQ and thus the biological inferiority of black people, the anger was plentiful. Geneticists and social scientists clamored to debunk Murray. Students and academics protested, and still do. But the book was readily available, even in airport bookstores. As a young man, I remember thinking how painful it must be as an African American traveler to see it sitting there in neat piles, on artful display. That wouldn't happen to Jews. A work alleging a genetic Jewish predilection for, well, anything would have been hounded into the underground. The closest analogue would be *The Israel Lobby and U.S. Foreign Policy*, by John Mearsheimer and Stephen Walt, which purported to document the power of the Israel lobby (heavily Jewish) and its efforts to skew American foreign policy toward Israel, even when that has run counter to American interests. But identifying the existence of a powerful foreign policy elite is a far cry from alleging a genetic inferiority.

Even sports team names could run a "Jewish test" that seems not to apply to, say, Native Americans. In my mind, the Jewish test of sports names runs as follows. The Atlanta Braves could possibly survive as the Jewish equivalent, the Atlanta

Maccabees, a fierce tribe of Biblical Jewish warriors, though replacing the silly Tomahawk Chop with the Maccabee daven wouldn't cut it. The Cleveland Indians have survived their fair share of protests. The Cleveland Jews? Unthinkable. The team's mascot, a foolishly grinning Chief Wahoo, has been roundly denounced by Native American activists as an ugly Stepin Fetchit caricature, yet he lives on. Now imagine a hook-nosed, cartoonish Hasid on a baseball cap. The Washington Redskins can bumble on, hated for their name and their owner's incompetence. The Washington Kikes? Are you kidding me? No, anti-Semitism doesn't get to flourish out in the open like that.

When anti-Semitism flares, it is usually inflamed by people who don't know Jews all that well, if at all. They look around and see groups not their own rising in stature or power or just numbers: Italians or Irish in past eras, blacks or Hispanics now, people the bigots feel superior to but somehow beaten by. How could these people who are so beneath us be beating us? the bigots ask, and begin to look for some unseen power orchestrating their decline: "white genocide." Invariably, they latch on to the Jews, the Other, all powerful yet weak and conniving. For most people, even the most bigoted, this was a conspiratorial hate that was spoken only in whispers, if at all.

Sure, there were organizations designed to separate the religions, Young Life, Fellowship of Christian Athletes—these met in our public school. Jewish organizations like B'nai B'rith and Young Judaea met elsewhere. All were basically designed to get young Christian girls dating young Christian boys, and young Jewish boys dating young Jewish girls. Once, when I went to a rustic leadership weekend conclave for a school service group, Interact, I uncomfortably sat around a campfire as the other teens passed around a New Testament, reading the teachings of Christ. I gathered my courage, and when the Bible reached me, I closed it and declared, "This is a service organization, not a religious organization," then walked off into the night. I not-so-bravely sneaked away and slept in an empty cabin, away from the other guys.

But generally I lived comfortably and forgetfully in suburbia, protected by subtlety, where open hate was someone else's problem. I'm not proud of that.

This was, I now know, a bit of childish, willful ignorance. Anti-Semitism tends to be invisible until it isn't. My father practiced medicine in Marietta, now an affluent Atlanta suburb but back then, in the 1970s, its own real Southern town. Long before my father's trip south, another Jew raised in New York had found himself in Georgia as a young man. Leo Frank, an engineer by training, of Cornell pedigree, came to Atlanta to help run the National Pencil Company, where his uncle was a director. He joined the most prominent Reform synagogue in the city, the Temple, built as a church-like edifice on Peachtree Street, with its sweeping front lawn, pews, organ, and choir. The rabbi, David Marx, had darkly noted, "In isolated instances there is no prejudice entertained for the individual Jew, but there exists widespread and deep-seated prejudice against Jews as an entire people."

On April 26, 1912, a thirteen-year-old girl named Mary Phagan, newly laid off from her fifty-five-hours-a-week job inserting eraser tips into the metal sleeves at the ends of National Pencil Company pencils, went to claim back wages of $1.20. The next morning, her battered, raped, and strangled body was found by the night watchman. Evidence, from the semiliterate "death notes" supposedly written by the victim to a pile of human shit deposited near the body, pointed to a janitor, Jim Conley, as the perpetrator. But police arrested the Jewish factory superintendent, Leo Frank, for the crime. The twists and turns of the prosecution, anti-Semitic slanders, and allegations of Frank's sexual predations eventually led to his conviction. Judge Leonard S. Roan sentenced him to death. The prosecutors had been determined to pin the heinous crime on a perpetrator far worse and more sinister than the barely educated black man suspected of it. For Victorian Atlanta, they portrayed Frank as a bizarre alien with exotic, Northern sexual predilections. Conley had titillated and scandalized the city with his testimony: "I have seen him in the office two or three times before Thanksgiving and a lady was in his office, and she was sitting down in a chair and she had her clothes up to here, and he was down on his knees."

Outside, populist politician and publisher Tom Watson used his own magazine to whip up anti-Semitic hysteria. The case was appealed all the way to the Supreme Court, where the conviction was upheld 7–2.

The governor of Georgia, John M. Slaton—convinced that Conley's eyewitness testimony against Frank was a lie from start to finish—commuted Frank's sentence to life in prison. Conley had admitted that "the shit in the shaft" (as it has come to be known) had been his, pretty strong evidence that he had been in the basement with the body. The good citizens of Georgia were outraged at the commutation, and Watson fanned the anger with his "Official Record in the Case of Leo M. Frank, Jew Pervert" and his epic screed against the "rich Jews" who had indicted the good State of Georgia with their outrageous efforts to finance Frank's defense. Watson burned and hanged Slaton in effigy, but he wanted Frank dead.

"Let no man reproach the South with Lynch law: let him remember the provocation; and let him say whether Lynch law *is not better than no law at all*," Watson thundered.

A former governor, a president of the Georgia Senate, and the mayor of Marietta organized the Knights of Mary Phagan and openly plotted the abduction and lynching of Leo Frank. Four weeks after the commutation, a fellow inmate slit Frank's throat with a butcher knife. Another prisoner, a surgeon, saved his life. Frank somehow remained hopeful that the campaign being waged in his behalf in the North, most prominently by the publisher of the *New York Times*, Adolph Ochs, would liberate him.

In early August 1915, Watson delivered his own sentence

in all caps: "THE NEXT JEW WHO DOES WHAT FRANK DID IS GOING TO GET EXACTLY THE SAME THING WE GIVE NEGRO RAPISTS."

On the afternoon of August 17, 1915, seven carloads of armed men told their wives they were going on a fishing trip and headed out of Marietta. Mechanics and telephone linemen, a doctor, a lawyer, and a preacher took different back roads to escape detection. Some wore goggles. Others didn't much care. They reconvened 150 miles from Marietta, outside the Georgia State Prison Farm in Milledgeville, where Leo Frank still lay in bed. They cut telephone lines, handcuffed a compliant warden, pushed aside the prison guards, and dragged Frank to a grove near Frey's Gin on the outskirts of Marietta. There, they strung him up with a rope supplied by a former Cobb County sheriff.

After a mob gathered around the body to pose for photos and mutilate the corpse, Fiddlin' John Carson took out his violin in Marietta Square and performed his "Ballad of Little Mary Phagan."

Little Mary Phagan
She went to work one day;
She went to the pencil factory
To get her weekly pay.

Leo Frank he met her
With a brutely heart and grin;

He says to little Mary,
"You'll never see home again."

Judge Roan passed the sentence;
He passed it very well;
The Christian doers of heaven
Sent Leo Frank to hell.

The site of the lynching is around the corner from the towering Big Chicken, a vintage Kentucky Fried Chicken and Cobb County's most famous landmark, just down the road from what would become White Water, the water park I used to go to as a kid, and about two and a half miles from my father's office near Kennestone Hospital, where patients once bartered chickens and mechanical services for his cardiac care in the 1970s and 1980s. The contrite citizens of Georgia eventually erected a plaque there, next to a Waffle House that sits on Roswell Road, in front of a down-at-heel Sears Outlet and a thrift store, across the street from El Huarache Veloz Taqueria, to mark the site of Leo Frank's lynching. But the plaque has been lost to the construction of a new off-ramp from Interstate 75. The eventual release of the lynching party roster was greeted with angry umbrage from the people of Marietta, who found the reckoning nothing but rude. Let bygones be bygones. Greater Atlanta wants to move on.

But scars remain. After proudly posing with Leo Frank's corpse, its neck gruesomely snapped, the good men of Georgia retired to the top of Stone Mountain, where they burned a cross and proclaimed the rebirth of the Ku Klux Klan. Frank's killers were well known, but there was no effort to bring any of them to justice.

The lynching of Leo Frank, known only vaguely to me as a child, was a landmark moment for the Jews of America—it prompted the founding of the Anti-Defamation League—and, more important, for the Jews of Atlanta and the city's proud black leadership. Frank's lawyers maintained that Jim Conley, the black janitor at the factory, was the killer, and in the decades after the trial, researchers who secured Frank's ultimate pardon have said that was likely so. To convict a Yankee Jew, the prosecutors had the delicate task of relying on a black man's testimony in front of an all-white Southern jury. They portrayed Conley as a simple man, too stupid to have made up the complicated story that hung the murder around Frank's neck, a story that involved Frank dictating a practically illiterate "murder note" to Conley to frame the night watchman who had discovered the body.

Though an African American janitor had helped convict a Jewish factory manager, the spectacle of a lynching—a horror so well known to Southern blacks—and the reemergence of the Klan bonded a shell-shocked Jewish community to Atlanta's black leadership. The civil rights movement was still decades away, but the Jews had their Emmett Till. In the wake of Leo Frank's lynching, half of Georgia's Jewish population of three thousand left the state. Those who remained assimilated further and shrunk from the political world. The Temple, my synagogue, did away with *chuppahs* at weddings. Services were practically Episcopalian. Rabbi Marx encouraged the low-profile bunker mentality. The Jews of Atlanta had hardly risen to the challenge of brutal anti-Semitism. They had cowered.

What followed in the 1920s and 1930s was perhaps the darkest age for American Jewry, a period of fear and menace— and also a precursor to the Trump era, when again a swirl of anti-immigrant fervor has been laced with anti-Semitic undertones. In his *Dearborn Independent*, Henry Ford railed against the Jewish financiers who, in his imagination, had orchestrated World War I. In 1920, Ford's newspaper began serializing "The International Jew." Over eighteen months, it all spilled out: "proof" that the Jews controlled international finance, even as they organized radical movements and manipulated diplomacy to send Christian men to their deaths in war. The Jews were the "international nation"—a high offense. It was Ford who took it upon himself to widely disseminate the fabricated *Protocols of the Elders of Zion* to prove to the nation that the Jewish conspiracy of world domination was real and active. And though he later claimed he was "mortified" to learn that the *Protocols* were a hoax, he never repented for his views. Just before his death in 1947, he proclaimed that Jewish bankers had orchestrated World War II.

Ford's *Dearborn Independent* was followed by Father Charles Edward Coughlin's hate-filled radio broadcasts of the 1930s, where he spread his sympathies for Hitler and Mussolini as the antidote to international Jewry. His magazine *Social Justice* reprinted the fraudulent *Protocols* in 1938. Like so many anti-Semites to follow, Father Coughlin took great umbrage at the label: "I want the good Jews with me, and I'm called a Jew baiter, an anti-Semite." When radio stations finally began refusing his broadcasts, his minions made it clear where they stood—and where they were convinced he stood. "Send Jews back where they came from in their leaky boats," they screamed during protests in New York. "Wait until Hitler comes over here." Followers tended to strip the artifice away from their leaders' couched rhetoric and let the world in on exactly what they were hearing.

In the halls of Congress, in state legislatures, and at colleges and universities, such hate had real impact. The anti-immigration laws of 1921 and 1924 were at least in part aimed at Jews, imposing strict quotas on Eastern European nations with large Jewish populations—the Muslim ban of their time. The Johnson-Reed Act of 1924 may have been no more explicit than President Trump's attempt to ban travel from six Muslim-majority nations, but the impact was clear: 86 percent of the permitted entries into the United States each year would be from Northern European countries, with Germany, Britain, and Ireland gaining the most visas. Jewish immigration slowed to a trickle.

Beyond the government, Harvard announced in 1922 that it would impose quotas on Jewish students, an overt plan that would be dropped, then enforced *de facto*, if not *de jure*, in elite institutions of higher education throughout the country. To its admissions categories of "character," "solidity," and "physical characteristics," Yale added a legacy preference in 1925 to keep its blue blood from mingling too much with Jew blood.

A 1938 poll found that 60 percent of the American public held Jews in low esteem, calling them greedy, dishonest, and pushy. A 1939 Roper poll for *Fortune* magazine found that only 39 percent of Americans saw Jews as worthy of being treated like other people; 53 percent said, "Jews are different and should be restricted."

The avowedly pro-Nazi America First Committee fed off the sentiment. Its most prominent spokesperson was Charles Lindbergh, an American hero no less beloved than Henry Ford. Lindbergh told an America First rally on September 11, 1941, that three forces were driving the nation toward war: Roosevelt, the British, and the Jews. "We must limit to a reasonable amount the Jewish influence," the aviator wrote in a portion of his diaries that was initially held back from publication. "Whenever the Jewish percentage of total population becomes too high, a reaction seems to invariably occur. It is too bad because a few Jews of the right type are, I believe, an asset to any country." When candidate Trump picked up Lindbergh's "America First" slogan, he may not have understood its historical import. It came, after all, in an interview with *New York Times* reporters when one of them, David Sanger, offhandedly asked if his foreign policy could be described as "America First." Why yes, it could, the candidate responded. But two years later Trump was still using it, despite what must have been hundreds of reminders of how Jewish voters heard those words.

As the flow of Jewish immigrants was choked off in the 1930s, the Jews of America grew to be dominated by a second generation of "alrightniks," eager to blend in and venture out of their all-Jewish neighborhoods, but not so eager to confront the injustices around them. They became Democrats, aligning themselves with the party of New Deal internationalism—but quietly. In a July 1938 *Fortune* magazine poll, Americans were asked, "What is your attitude towards allowing German, Austrian and other political refugees to come to the United States?" Sixty-seven percent said, "With conditions as they are, we should try to keep them out." In January 1939, well after *Kristallnacht*, Gallup's American Institute of Public Opinion asked, "It has been proposed to bring to this country 10,000 refugee children from Germany—most of them Jewish—to be taken care of in American homes. Should the government permit these children to come in?"

Thirty percent said yes; 61 percent, no. The bill to allow those refugee children quietly died, with the help of the Roosevelt administration. "It would be inadvisable to raise the question of increasing quotas or radical changes in our immigration laws," Undersecretary of State Sumner Welles offered, fearing antagonizing nativists in Congress as President Roosevelt nudged the country toward war. Certainly, news of the persecution of Jews in Nazi Germany had reached American newspapers, although the breadth of the slaughter was still largely unknown, or at least unpublicized by the Roosevelt government. To many Americans, those ships harboring desperate Jewish refugees and sailing the Eastern seaboard in their fruitless search of a port could actually be harboring German spies or Communists—but never would-be Americans.

This anti-immigrant sentiment sounds familiar, of course; the word "Jewish" from the polls of yesteryear sounds in context very much like "Muslim" today, as "Germany" echoes off "Syria" or "Yemen." The notion that a whole class of people must be excluded to avoid the theoretical entry of one enemy is repeating itself today. It was Donald Trump Jr. who, on August 13, took to social media during the presidential campaign to broadcast the image of a bowl of candy with the question, "If I had a bowl of skittles [*sic*] and I told you just three would kill you. [*sic*] Would you take a handful? That's our Syrian refugee problem." He added: "This image says it all. Let's end the politically correct agenda that doesn't put America first."

I wouldn't be so bold as to suggest that the president's son was familiar with the Nazi-era children's book *The Poisonous Mushroom*. But members of the alt-right did not miss the parallel between the parable of the Skittles and the lesson of the mushroom, published in 1938:

> Look, Franz, human beings in this world are like the mushrooms in the forest. There are good mushrooms and there are good people. There are poisonous, bad mushrooms and there are bad people. And we have to be on our guard against bad people just as we have against poisonous mushrooms. Do you understand that?
>
> Franz slaps his chest in pride: Of course I know, mother! They are the Jews!

And just as Trump Jr.'s tweet—one of so many—was not enough to rouse the nation in 2016, the news from Germany in the 1930s was not enough to wake the Jews of America— "the Jews of Silence," as Elie Wiesel would later call us when the plight of Soviet Jewry elicited similar indifference.

During the rise of Hitler, the American Jewish Committee, representing the more affluent and assimilated German Jewish community, promoted quiet advocacy and diplomacy to counter Nazism. The American Jewish Congress, the redoubt of more recent Eastern European arrivals, wanted a brasher approach: rallies, demonstrations, and direct pressure on the Roosevelt administration. Rabbis warned widely of the darkness descending on European Jewry. Rallies were staged; signs were carried. But to many American Jews, silence was the response. Why attract attention when avowed anti-Semites like

Charles Lindbergh and Henry Ford occupied such prominent places in American society? Why rock the boat and risk the same fate as European Jewry? Better to be Americans first. As in so many other moments in American and world history, American Jewry, when facing an existential threat, just couldn't get it together.

The borders thickened. Nationalism rose. The drawbridge rose. The Jew did not flourish.

It is hard for us to understand now, but it would take decades for the Holocaust Over There to become part of the American Jewish story. In 1961, the Israelis insisted on a public, televised trial for Adolf Eichmann, one of the architects of the genocide, to engage a world that very much wanted to forget. It was not until that decade that the Holocaust actually became a seminal event in human history, separate and apart from the other horrors of World War II.

But before American Jewry accepted the Holocaust as its touchstone of dread, before "Never Again" was uttered in unison on the western shore of the Atlantic, an awakening emerged from the ashes of World War II. Around the globe and at home, the walls of isolation began coming down—and as the walls descended, America's Jews and blacks found each other.

On *erev* Yom Kippur 1947, with the survivors of Auschwitz and Treblinka still living in displaced-persons camps in Europe, Rabbi Jacob Rothschild ascended to the pulpit-like *bima* in the sanctuary of the Temple to decry segregation in the Deep South. He had already rejected some of the changes adopted by Rabbi Marx in the wake of the Frank lynching, reinstating Jewish traditions and encouraging congregants to observe the laws of the Torah, assimilation be damned. (He would famously utter, "There is too much 'bar' and not enough 'mitzvah' in our celebrations.") But it was his outspoken support of racial integration and the civil rights movement that attracted outsiders' attention. He had seen combat at Guadalcanal during World War II, the first Jewish chaplain to come under fire in that war. The Japanese had not frightened him; nor could the bigots of the South. He was a proud and open supporter of Martin Luther King.

Then combat came to him.

In the early hours of October 12, 1958, when no one was inside, a group of white supremacists calling themselves the Confederate Underground exploded fifty sticks of dynamite in a recessed doorway at the Temple. This time, there was no celebratory cross burning, no march in Klan robes. Atlanta's mayor, William Hartsfield, rushed to the Temple to declare, "Whether they like it or not, every political rabble-rouser is the godfather of these cross burners and dynamiters who sneak around in the dark and give a bad name to the South. It is high time the decent people of the South rise and take charge."

Rabbi Rothschild's sermon that Friday was titled "And None Shall Make Them Afraid": "This despicable act has made brighter the flame of courage and renewed in splendor the fires of determination and dedication. It has reached the hearts of men everywhere and roused the conscience of a people united in righteousness. All of us together shall rear from the rubble of devastation a city and a land in which all men are truly brothers and none shall make them afraid."

Ralph McGill, the editor of the *Atlanta Constitution* who would win a Pulitzer Prize the following year, wrote in 1958 the words of the reemergent citizen of the world, where identity is both universal and nonexistent: "You do not preach and encourage hatred for the Negro and hope to restrict it to that field. . . . When the wolves of hate are loosed on one people, then no one is safe."

With the ashes of the crematoria still in the topsoil of Europe, such sentiment would seem self-evident: hate begets hate, and no one is safe as it flourishes. But of course it wasn't. It took effort to see the hate that Martin Luther King and Ralph Abernathy marched against as kin to the genocidal prejudices of the Nazis, to understand that Operation Wetback, undertaken by the Eisenhower administration to deport undocumented Mexican immigrants in 1954, could legitimize intolerance, prejudice, and the kind of hate that could stack dynamite against the walls of a synagogue a few years later. The unity of the dispossessed seemed elusive, until it wasn't.

The alliance between black and Jewish leaders in the 1950s and 1960s gave rise to the notion that America could—and would—move forward, seemingly inexorably, toward that enlightened place where Judaism wouldn't matter, where the lynch mob's rope and the Klansman's dynamite would be rendered useless forever.

Toward safe, self-satisfied complacency.

The Jewish political reemergence during the civil rights movement was profound. Julius Rosenwald, chairman of Sears, Roebuck & Company, teamed with Booker T. Washington and local African American leaders to create black schools throughout the South. Rabbi Ira Sanders testified in Little Rock against segregation legislation. Rabbi Arthur Lelyveld was beaten as he marched in Hattiesburg. A quarter to a third of all Freedom Riders who came to the South to register black voters were Jewish. Reform rabbis heeded Martin Luther King's call in 1964 to gather in St. Augustine, Florida, where they endured taunts and arrest, acting as decoys while black demonstrators desegregated motel swimming pools. The Klan bombed Rabbi Perry Nussbaum's synagogue in Jackson, Mississippi, in 1967, then, two months later, bombed his house. Donors, lawyers, champions in Congress, and white leaders of the civil rights movement were disproportionately Jewish. Michael Schwerner and Andrew Goodman, two young Jewish idealists, joined a young black Mississippian named James Chaney on a Freedom Ride to register African Americans to vote and were murdered by the Klan on June 21, 1964. In March of the following year, African American civil rights leaders John Lewis,

Ralph Abernathy, the Reverend Martin Luther King Jr., and the Reverend Fred Shuttlesworth linked arms with a white man, Rabbi Abraham Joshua Heschel, to lead the march over the Edmund Pettus Bridge in Selma and on to Montgomery.

Such sacrifice helped cement a powerful role for Jews in the Democratic Party that stretched back to the New Deal. Senators like Abraham Ribicoff of Connecticut, Herbert Lehman of New York, and Howard Metzenbaum of Ohio came and went without much fuss over their religion, as did Bella Abzug, Tony Beilenson, Ed Koch, and Edward Mezvinsky in the House. In 2000 Al Gore named as his running mate Joe Lieberman, an Orthodox Jew who observed the Sabbath. There was hardly a ripple. The United States came within a few hundred disputed votes in Florida of having a Jewish vice president, and no one even mentioned that Lieberman's place on the Democratic ticket had anything to do with Gore's defeat. There were plenty of other, more obvious culprits. The Jewish community dared to ask whether anti-Semitism was really dead.

But it was when Jewish Democrats were joined by Jewish Republicans that American Jewry could really relax. Arlen Specter, Norm Coleman, Rudy Boschwitz—suddenly Jews really were bipartisan, our presence not confined to House districts and states with high Jewish populations. In Minnesota, where the Jewish population is 1.45 percent, a Democrat, Paul Wellstone, was followed to the Senate by a Republican,

Norm Coleman, who was then defeated by a Democrat, Al Franken—all Jewish. Wisconsin, with a Jewish population of 0.8 percent, at one time had two Jewish senators, Russ Feingold and Herb Kohl. Dan Glickman represented the now deepred House district around Wichita, Kansas.

Rahm Emanuel and Eric Cantor raced to become the first Jewish speaker of the House, and no one screamed, no one threatened or fumed or blew anything up. No one cared.

In early 2011, the *Forward* greeted Emanuel's election as mayor of the nation's third-largest city with the headline "Chicago Picks First Jewish Mayor. Ho Hum."

Chicago magazine needled Mayor Emanuel later that year when it gushed, "For Cantor, the first Jewish majority leader—and the only Jewish Republican in either the House or Senate, the dream of becoming the first Jewish Speaker is very much alive. Some observers see his Speakership as a pit stop en route to becoming the first Jewish president, but others say he doesn't have what it takes to reach the White House."

If anything, the two political parties battled each other over which one loved Israel more, stood most firmly for Judeo-Christian values (the Judeo part got added somewhere along the way), and was friendlier and more inviting to Jewish voters (and Jewish donors).

Then, in 2008, the bottom dropped out. A decade later, it is remarkable how we have forgotten how scary the financial crisis was, when capitalism itself seemed to be on the brink.

Bear Stearns, Merrill Lynch, Lehman Brothers, AIG, Fannie Mae, Freddie Mac—if they weren't rescued by the government, they collapsed. Hundreds of thousands lost their jobs each month during a horrifying stretch from April 2009 to December 2009. Unemployment soared so high and so suddenly that talk of a depression seemed not like fearmongering but rather simple historical relativism. The magnitude of the Great Recession, the sustained job losses, stock market declines, evaporation of wealth, and closings of businesses had no comparison to any stretch other than 1929. Barack Obama, the first African American president, came to power as Americans legitimately questioned the future of democratic capitalism.

And where was the hate? Sure, there were voters who could not bring themselves to pull the lever for a black man with a strange name, but as Obama himself said countless times, his skin color probably was, on net, a benefit. More people came out to vote for the first black president than secreted themselves into the booth to vote against him because of the color of his skin. Blacks who had never, or rarely, voted came out in droves. I covered the Obama campaign in 2008, first for the *Washington Post* and then for the *Wall Street Journal*. I watched more than a hundred thousand people throng central Indianapolis to see Obama speak just before Election Day; saw a carnival of joy in Miami; followed him through southern Missouri and Richmond and Leesburg, Virginia; and watched him play pool—badly—in Charleston, West

Virginia. I saw no white hoods or green Pepe the Frog memes. I saw pride, even among the people who would ultimately vote against him.

And from the moment he was inaugurated, Barack Obama made clear that the drawbridges would remain down as his administration struggled to right the ship of liberal democracy. Obama was a proud, outspoken internationalist, and the world community responded. Londoners thronged the streets to catch a glimpse as he huddled with world leaders at the Group of Twenty summit in 2009, trying to coordinate an international response to the growing economic crisis. "In an age where our economies are linked more closely than ever before, the whole world has been touched by this devastating downturn. And today, the world's leaders have responded," Obama declared at the close of the summit.

People packed Castle Square in Prague to hear the new American president call for a world without nuclear weapons: "I'm speaking to you in the center of a Europe that is peaceful, united and free—because ordinary people believed that divisions could be bridged, even when their leaders did not. They believed that walls could come down; that peace could prevail." They lined the streets of Ankara and Istanbul, and filled lecture halls in Beijing and Cairo. At Egypt's Al-Azhar University, he declared: "When a financial system weakens in one country, prosperity is hurt everywhere. When a new flu infects one human being, all are at risk. When one nation pursues a nuclear weapon, the risk of nuclear attack rises for all nations. When violent extremists operate in one stretch of mountains, people are endangered across an ocean."

The Right grumbled about "apology tours" and Kenyan socialism, weakness abroad and leading from behind, but internationalism didn't miss a beat. There seemed to be hardly a whiff of rising ethno-nationalism.

We had weathered the greatest economic crisis since 1929, lost more jobs, more wealth, and more certainty than in a dozen previous recessions, and we were still standing. The borders were still blurred. Nationalism and chauvinism were in check. Undocumented immigrants marched in the streets of Washington and Los Angeles demanding rights. The polyglot nation recovered.

Barack Obama was the apotheosis of liberal internationalism. A Jew was White House chief of staff. An American president held a Passover seder, then another. The Jew thrived.

In late March 2016, at a very bad Thai restaurant in the little town of Selfoss, Iceland, I and my daughters Alissa and Hannah sat with my girlfriend, Jennifer, and her daughters Sadie and Hannah (yes, two Hannahs) as Jennifer and I pressed forward with the difficult task of family blending. Jennifer's Hannah was talking about Black Lives Matter and the injustices that befall African Americans every day.

"Anti-Semitism basically doesn't exist in the United States," she asserted.

I shocked myself with my response. I recoiled at her words and argued passionately that Jews must never think that anti-Semitism has been eradicated. Vigilance, I preached. The Jew can never be at peace.

I sounded like my grandmother.

TWO

The Israel Deception

In the summer of 2015, after the United States, Russia, Britain, France, and Germany struck their deal with Iran to dismantle its nuclear program, Representative Jerrold Nadler, a Jewish Democrat who represents the ritzier parts of Manhattan, along with some enclaves of Orthodox Jewry that are decidedly un-ritzy, was attacked so viciously for his support of the nuclear deal that the Anti-Defamation League was moved to denounce the hate.

"No matter one's politics or views on the Iran deal, vicious, ad hominem attacks are unacceptable in any circumstance. Political leaders, opinion leaders, and public figures across the spectrum should set an example by rejecting such rhetoric and forcefully speaking out against language that dehumanizes," the group wrote.

Three Jewish representatives who opposed the Iran nuclear

deal also spoke out: "Vitriolic rhetoric and threats distract from the thoughtful debate this important issue deserves and, in some cases, unacceptably perpetuate hate," wrote Eliot Engel, Nita Lowey, and Steve Israel.

And who was perpetrating all this hatred against a Jew? Jews.

"Stinking kapo," one commenter wrote on Nadler's Facebook page, equating his support for a hard-fought, complex agreement between six nations to the collaboration of Jews with Nazis in the concentration camps. "When you die there [*sic*] no place for you on [*sic*] Jewish cemetery," another assailant wrote.

The Jewish community was so riven that major Jewish organizations tried to avoid the subject of the Iran deal. Taking a position would be too risky—to donors and rank-and-file members. Conversation could not be constructive.

I had my own brush with fratricidal Jew-on-Jew violence during that heated debate. I had sat down with a young graphic designer at the *Times* to try to figure out which Democrats in Congress were breaking with Obama to oppose the deal. The traits of such defectors were fairly obvious: they were naturally to the right end of the Democratic spectrum; their districts were either in the Greater New York or Miami area; their districts were heavily Jewish, or they themselves were Jewish— match two or three of those traits and you probably were going to vote against the Iran deal. We published those characteristics in a basic rows-and-columns grid, identifying each Democrat who had come out against the Iran deal and which characteristics applied. Needless to say, none of the lawmakers identified in the graphic as Jewish had been "outed": they had identified themselves as Jewish and cited their faith as they pronounced their opposition. The *Times* had even had the audacity to color each column with a splash of yellow—an allusion, so we thought, to a highlighter pen, but in the minds of our detractors, we were using Holocaust Star of David coloring.

The ensuing uproar struck me as absurd, and I am still hearing about it. The first round of attacks was aimed at the designer who put together the grid. Seeing her roundly blasted on social media as an anti-Semite, I spoke up, saying that I had identified the characteristics of a no-voting Democrat and had supervised the construction of the graphic. That unleashed the torrent. I was called an anti-Semite and accused of outing members of Congress and presiding over a "Jew tracker." When I responded, hey, I'm Jewish, I got the kapo epithet and the tag "self-hating Jew." I didn't take it too seriously. I used the notoriety to plug my novel *No. 4 Imperial Lane*, which was still pretty fresh on the bookshelves of the few bookstores then still in existence. What surprises me is the longevity of the controversy. A year later, when I was under attack by neo-Nazis and alt-right white nationalists, I got a call from a reporter at the *Atlanta Jewish Times*. One of his first questions was, "How does it feel to be on the other side after you printed that anti-Semitic chart?"

In truth, the searing debate in the Jewish community over the Iran deal had nothing to do with anti-Semitism. Two of the lead American negotiators, Wendy Sherman and Adam Szubin, were Jewish—Szubin a *kippa*-wearing Orthodox. It was about Israel, and more specifically about Israel's conservative prime minister, Binyamin Netanyahu, who vociferously opposed the nuclear agreement and preached his opposition in apocalyptic terms. Never mind that senior members of Israeli intelligence supported it, on the record and in public. Never mind that the Israeli public was split, or that the conclusion of the agreement was accompanied by yet another dramatic round of arms sales and technical military assistance to Israel. Bibi was opposed. And who knew Israel's best interests better than Bibi? Were you with him or against him? American Jewry was split between the tribalists and the internationalists: those who saw the Jew's role primarily as falling in behind the leader of the tribe and those who saw Israel in the larger context of international relations and global security.

Embedded in both sides of the angry Jewish debate was the freighted question, Which camp supported Israel more?

For years now, it has been the only question in the Jewish political world: Where do you stand on Israel?

The official support for Israel in the United States has been steady and strong since the dawn of the Jewish state. In 1948, at the founding of Israel, American Jewry itself was divided on the degree of support we should lend it. There were ardent Zionists, especially among the Orthodox (though one sect of Hasidim is vehemently anti-Zionist, believing that only God could consecrate a Jewish state). There were opponents of Zionism among Reform Jews. There was a lot of indifference, as America settled into that great age of complacency, the 1950s, when American superiority was unquestioned, Europe and Japan were still cleaning up the rubble, and Jews could afford silence. It was not until Israel's near-miraculous triumph in the Six-Day War in 1967, with its iconic image of young, beautiful Israeli soldiers beholding the Wailing Wall for the first time, that Israel captivated the Jewish mind. It was not until the Yom Kippur War of 1973, when a surprise attack by united Arab forces very nearly overran the Jewish state, that Israel and Israel's security began developing into a singular obsession.

Since then, there have been occasional rumblings of discontent, some concern for the amount of treasure spent on aid and military matériel, and chagrin on the Left over the treatment of Palestinians. Certainly on college campuses, anti-Zionist sentiment and support for the BDS movement (boycott, divestment, and sanctions) should not be understated. But the images of anti-Israel protesters in Europe marching with signs that contort Stars of David into swastikas are jarring to the American eye. Beyond political correctness on some college campuses, anti-Israel sentiment still has no strong purchase in the American political or social scene.

In 1973 and 1974, during the Arab oil embargo, there were voices on the right that questioned whether the American tilt toward Israel was worth it. The Arab oil producers withheld their fuel from the United States to punish Washington for its support of Israel during the Yom Kippur War. Europe and Canada responded with a foreign-policy shift toward the oil producers. Israel's democratic socialist government, with its national health care, collectivist kibbutzim, and slightly less collectivist *moshavim*, didn't seem quite kosher to some on the American right. Yet Washington stayed steadfastly in the Israeli camp, even as some voters—weary of gas lines, shortages, soaring prices at the pump, and shrinking cars—wanted a change.

Those rumbles on the right were silenced not by Republican foreign-policy graybeards but by Jerry Falwell's founding in 1979 of the Moral Majority, the herald of the Christian right. "To stand against Israel is to stand against God," Falwell declared. Pat Robertson's *700 Club* extolled the virtues of the Jewish state, a redoubt of democratic ideals and Judeo-Christian values in a sea of Muslims. Christian tourism in the Holy Land brought a steady stream of Middle America to that small island of recognizable civilization in the Middle East, about the size of New Jersey. Amid M16-wielding Israeli soldiers and wary Palestinians, pilgrims from Wisconsin and Kansas wearing Bermuda shorts and church-issued matching T-shirts carried crosses through the Old City of Jerusalem, tracing Jesus's path on the Via Dolorosa.

Savvy Jewish leaders understood that this affection for Israel was not exactly geopolitical. Christian fundamentalists saw the founding of the Jewish state and the ingathering of Jews in the Holy Land as an important step toward the New Testament's prophesied Armageddon and the eventual return of Jesus Christ. The Jews all might die, slaughtered in the battle of the faithful against the faithless, incinerated in the Tribulation or left behind by the Rapture—"How's it gonna end? Isn't gonna be none too pretty," Pat Robertson warned—but for now they were friends. The Jews would have to put up with some inconvenient theology—and some distasteful cultural appropriation—but it was in the service of the Jewish state. In 1981, after Israeli warplanes bombed a nuclear reactor in Iraq, Israeli prime minister Menachem Begin called Falwell to rally a favorable response from the American public. Thirty-six years later, a staunchly conservative congressman named Clay Higgins journeyed from his home state of Louisiana to the gas chambers of Auschwitz-Birkenau to videotape himself preaching the gospel of raised drawbridges. "It's hard to walk away from gas chambers and ovens without a very sober feeling of commitment, unwavering commitment, to make damn sure that the United States of America is protected from the evils of the world," Higgins intoned, not seeing the irony of a nationalist message filmed at the site of the National Socialists' greatest crime. The Jews largely held their tongues.

The Holocaust had its contemporary geopolitical purposes. Armageddon could wait.

As the Christian Right became increasingly smitten with the Jewish state, the two political parties in Washington fought over which one could support Israel more. There seemed to be no request for arms that went too far, no aid package too rich, no act of violence by the Israeli military too brutal, no act of kindness or reconciliation too insignificant to extol. Liberal Jewish Democrats like Eliot Engel, Brad Sherman, Howard Berman, and Rahm Emanuel turned to mush when the subject was Israel and its fight to survive and thrive. Jewish Republicans like Eric Cantor, Norm Coleman, and Lee Zeldin, smaller in number than their Democratic counterparts, used their faith to grow in stature, and their stature to argue for the immutability of the American-Israeli alliance. The annual American Israel Public Affairs Committee gathering in Washington became an exercise in kissing the ring, as the leading lights of both parties streamed onto the podium to deliver ever more bellicose professions of adoration.

AIPAC was understandable, in some sense: a single powerful organization devoted to cultivating the close bond between tiny Israel, vulnerable in a Middle East where every neighbor craved to drive it into the sea, and the one true superpower, the United States. But one by one, virtually every Jewish organization became enthralled with this same mission. The American Jewish Committee, the American Jewish Congress, the Jewish Federations of North America, the Conference of Presidents of Major American Jewish Organizations, the Zionist Organization of America, the World Zionist Organization, the Religious Zionists of America, the National Council of Young Israel—all spoke of, lobbied on, and raised money for Israel, Israel, Israel. Perhaps it was because as Jews secularized, becoming less and less grounded in actual religion, we had nothing else to talk about. Perhaps it was because for the donors of all these groups, Israel was the one common denominator, the tried-and-true theme of the little Israeli David squaring off against the giant Arab Goliath. Perhaps there was just too much else to fight about and we were done fighting.

Ken Stern, the executive director of the Justus and Karin Rosenberg Foundation, sees one big reason: money. For twenty-five years, Stern worked at the American Jewish committee, finishing his tenure as director of the Division on Anti-Semitism and Extremism. When he arrived, he recalled, the committee had an entire floor devoted to domestic issues: education, immigration, interethnic relations, and interreligious outreach. Over time, those concerns were subordinated to the singular focus on Israel. Clean energy? Okay, but make sure it relates to Israeli energy security. Interfaith efforts? Fine, as long as they are geared to heading off the boycott, divestment, and sanctions movement. Outreach to the Hispanic community? By all means; we must maintain good relations with a rising political force that needs to be kept on Israel's side. "When I got there, we had this deep concern about inner cities, poverty, so many issues, but those sort of withered away over time," Stern told me. The American Jewish Committee saw where the big money was. Why chase after $5,000 or $10,000 donations when hedge fund managers were cutting checks in six figures, or well into the millions? But to get the big money, the committee needed to be more tempered, more conservative—and more focused on Israel. There emerged a division of labor of sorts: If you had big bucks and wanted to press your pro-Israel sentiments on a member of Congress or an official in the White House, go to AIPAC. If you wanted to discuss it with a foreign minister or diplomat, the American Jewish Committee would take care of you.

Defenders of the committee say that is a bit exaggerated. The AJC still does some domestic work, even some not connected to Israel. But they concede it's basically right. David Harris, the committee's chief executive officer, was scarred by his work with the United Nations, at what he said was rank anti-Semitism that pervaded anti-Israel sentiments. And he took the committee in this direction as a moral imperative.

As for other organizations, well, we all have to have priorities. In 2014, after fifty-four years of supporting Jewish writers, filmmakers, artists, composers, choreographers, and scholars devoted to Jewish life in America, the National Foundation for Jewish Culture closed its doors for good. No need to support Jewish culture in the United States if that culture was focused squarely on a New Jersey–size nation on the Mediterranean Sea.

Beyond Washington, the Jewish political divide grew more pronounced, but the arguments were always over Israel. The acolytes of AIPAC saw it as an American Jewish responsibility to back the positions of the Israeli government, whether it be hard-right Likud or left-leaning Labor (though, to be sure, AIPAC always seemed to lean Likud). Israel as a nation became synonymous with the Israeli government. When control of the Knesset vacillated between center-left and center-right coalitions, that was broadly acceptable. But as the Likud grew more entrenched in Jerusalem and right-wing splinter parties pulled the government ever more rightward, a strain of liberalism among American Jews that emerged after the Six-Day War was fortified, urging support for nongovernmental organizations working for peace and Jewish-Palestinian understanding, despite the government's positions. The New Israel Fund, J Street, Americans for Peace Now, and other groups emerged to counter the power of AIPAC and the compliant mainline Jewish organizations. The Jews of the United States took sides, and they fought—incessantly. And it was always about Israel. It is just so much easier to focus on another country's problems when ours seem so intractable—no matter how intractable the other country's problems are.

Jewish identity, thousands of years in the making, seemed to increasingly boil down to one characteristic: affinity for the Jewish state. In an October 2013 Pew Research Center survey of American Jews, seven in ten said they feel very attached (30 percent) or somewhat attached (39 percent) to Israel. Nearly a quarter had visited Israel more than once. Forty percent said the land that is now Israel was given by God to the Jewish people—a remarkable number given that only 19 percent said being Jewish meant observing Jewish law. Forty-three percent of Jews said being a Jew meant caring about Israel, just behind being intellectually curious and just ahead or having a good sense of humor. *Oy.* Jewish philanthropists like Michael Steinhardt, Charles Bronfman, and Sheldon Adelson have pumped millions of dollars into Birthright Israel, which offers Jewish teens and young adults all-expenses paid trips to the Holy Land, no questions asked (though the Israeli government has asked that Jewish participants in the BDS movement be excluded). The vinyl banners in front of synagogues around the country once proclaimed "Remember Darfur." Now they read "We Stand with Israel."

And at what cost? The American Jewish obsession with Israel has taken our eyes off not only the politics of our own country, the growing gulf between rich and poor, and the rising tide of nationalism but also our own grounding in faith. As one rabbi told me, Jewish life should grow out of belief, faith, and history, not today's *New York Times.* We have grown reactive, responding to events or provocations rather than pursuing a spiritually driven mission to do as the Torah tells us: Welcome the stranger, for you were strangers in the Land of Egypt.

Jews have grown so obsessed with Israel that the overt and covert signals of anti-Semitism beamed from the interior of the Trump campaign appeared to be disregarded by people like Adelson and Bernie Marcus, the Home Depot co-founder and Republican mega-donor who seemed wowed by candidate Trump's solemn promise to immediately move the U.S. embassy from Tel Aviv to Jerusalem and to back Likud's expansive settlement policy on the West Bank. Never mind that both moves were purely symbolic: Netanyahu was going to do what he was going to do regardless of Washington's feckless policies or the location of its ambassador. What mattered was Israel, pure and simple.

It was something of a comeuppance when President Trump immediately backed off his promise of an embassy move, swiftly sent a letter to Prime Minister Netanyahu scolding him on settlements, and promised a new push for Israeli-Palestinian peace talks. But beyond leaked word that Adelson was really, really, really angry, no apologies or mea culpas were forthcoming from American Jewry. Trump did make Israel a stop on his first trip abroad—the earliest visit to the Jewish state by any American president. But before his arrival, his White House made no comment on the two Israeli-American journalists who were denied visas to follow the president into Saudi Arabia, where he happily danced with swords and his commerce secretary boasted that there had been no protestors.

Once he had landed in Jerusalem, Trump did note that he "just got back from the Middle East," a moment memorialized by Ron Dermer, Israel's ambassador to the United States, covering his face with his hand in frustration or amazement. Trump scheduled all of fifteen minutes for a stop at Yad Vashem, Israel's revered Holocaust memorial and museum, and in his brief remarks there—from 1:27 to 1:34 p.m.—he managed both to extol the Jewish people and let slip his cherished stereotypes: "Through persecution, oppression, death, and destruction, the Jewish people have persevered. They have thrived. They've become so successful in so many places." Ever solicitous, Netanyahu thanked the president, who "in so few words said so much." No one took note of the irony that the Holocaust survivor who greeted Trump, Margot Herschenbaum, had been rescued in 1939 by the *Kindertransport*, which had whisked her out of Germany and had saved thousands of other Jewish children. Refugees like Herschenbaum had been denied entry to the United States during World War II, just as Trump has steadfastly denied the entry of Syrian children fleeing war and death in their own country.

Trump returned the prime minister's obsequious fawning by declining to bring Netanyahu with him to the Western Wall, which, bizarrely, his government repeatedly refused to call part of Israel. As the entourage was leaving Riyadh, Trump's secretary of state, Rex Tillerson, a former ExxonMobil CEO clearly more at home with the Saudi sheiks, declared, "On to the second stop, Tel Aviv, home of Judaism." Perhaps he thought, well, it looks like Miami Beach, and a lot of Jews live there, too.

No matter. Trump's repeated declarations of unqualified support for the state of Israel was all anyone stateside seemed to want.

"The Obama administration gave us eight years of 'daylight' between the U.S. and Israel, a dangerous nuclear deal with Iran, and a set of policies that allowed terrorist groups to grow and thrive across the region. That era is over," a thankful Republican Jewish Coalition proclaimed as the president winged it to Europe.

For an older generation of Jews, the argument for an obsessive focus on Israel was always simple: the Holocaust proved that Jews needed their own state, a safe haven from the hate that could return at any time. That appeal meshed nicely with the twin obsessions of American Judaism, the Holocaust and Israel. When asked what it means to be Jewish, 73 percent of American Jewry answered "to remember the Holocaust."

But that argument ignores geopolitical and military reality: Israel is only as strong as the United States and its willingness to support Israel. Despite its technological sophistication and economic growth, Israel remains a tiny redoubt surrounded by forces that could overwhelm it by manpower alone. It is by far the largest recipient of American military aid. Israel's Iron Dome missile shield was built with Israeli ingenuity but also a lot of American help. Israeli engineers helped design the advanced F-35 Lightning II, and Israel's air force will be the only one in the Middle East to receive shipments of the fighter jet—part of Washington's continued commitment to keeping the Israeli Defense Forces' strategic advantage in the region. But when the plane rolls off the assembly line, that assembly line will be Lockheed Martin's, in Fort Worth, Texas, seven thousand miles from Tel Aviv. The fact is, the Jewish haven is safe only as long as it stays under the American security umbrella. American Jewry should be at least as focused on maintaining political support for Judaism in the United States as it is on sustaining Israel's security.

The stirrings of the BDS movement on American campuses is worrisome as much for what it says about the American Jew's inextricable links to Israel as for what it says about anti-Semitism. Anti-Israel sentiment is synonymous with anti-Semitism in the minds of so many people, both Jews and gentiles, because Israel has become synonymous with Judaism. When Rachel Beyda, a second-year economics major at the University of California, Los Angeles, sought a seat on the student council's judicial board, a member of the Undergraduate Students Association Council, Fabienne Roth, demanded, "Given that you are a Jewish student and very active in the Jewish community, how do you see yourself being able to maintain an unbiased view?" Considering the ritualistic appeals for diversity on college campuses and in workplaces, it was a remarkable question. Isn't a goal of diversity to have different viewpoints? It appeared that the Jewish viewpoint was not to be valued, but dig a little deeper and the concern wasn't so much Beyda's religion or American Jewish identity but somehow the assumption that being "very active in the Jewish community" translated to being very active in the promotion of Israeli government policies. Why? For God's sake, Beyda's Jewish bona fides stemmed largely from her leadership role in a Jewish sorority—hardly a hotbed for vehement Zionism.

For young progressives on campuses across the country, fealty to the BDS movement is just another item to check off as they make their way down the list of liberal causes: Black Lives Matter, immigrants' rights, LGBT rights, gender sensitivities, opposition to all manner of cultural appropriation, and intersectionality. Sympathizing with the oppressed is the job of the "woke" generation, but although Jews have been exiled, isolated, disenfranchised, and massacred since Nebuchadnezzar, we are no more due the sympathies of the Left on campus than we are due special treatment in higher education admissions or workplace hiring. We're just doing too darned well, as Trump noted in Israel. To the advocates of BDS, Israel's current military strength and right-wing policies negate three thousand years of hatred.

In the summer of 2017, three Jewish participants in the Chicago "Dyke March"—an alternative gay pride parade deemed less corporatist than the main event—were asked to leave the festivities because they were waving a rainbow flag with a Jewish star on it—what they called a "Jewish Pride" flag. "It was a flag from my congregation which celebrates my queer, Jewish identity which I have done for over a decade marching in the Dyke March with the same flag," Laurel Grauer told the *Windy City Times*. This time around, she said, she lost count of the number of people who harassed her. Why? Apparently the presence of a Star of David "made people feel unsafe." After all, Chicago's Dyke March Collective is "anti-Zionist" and "pro-Palestinian," organizers said. The message: even Jews who are not single-mindedly obsessed with the endless battles over Israel can't escape them. We've been tagged, whether we like it or not.

American Jews are still loath to see it, but the Israel diversion is proving to be a trap. Zionism—Jewish nationalism—cuts both ways. Anti-Semites in Europe—and in some quarters of American academia—maintain that they have nothing against Jews per se. Jewish suffering through the ages can do nothing but inspire compassion, the European anti-Semites are careful to say. The reality of the Holocaust should not be questioned, though to be fair, they might add, the suffering at Auschwitz was no more and no less cruel than the death of Palestinian children in Gaza, the attempted annihilation of Turkish Armenians that gave the world the term "genocide," the slaughter of Bosnian Muslims, or the butchering of Rwandan Tutsi. Death is death. We shouldn't be in the business of elevating one atrocity over another. It is Israel, they say, that is illegitimate: a colonial, racist state injected into the Middle East by Western powers reeling from guilt over the death of the 6 million. Sadly, European intellectuals say, the Jews have used the Holocaust as a moral bludgeon to justify all manner of evil deeds by the illegitimate Jewish state, and for that we can have no tolerance.

And that intolerance has led many in Europe—and some in the American academy and fringe left—to make a dangerous leap: the Jews in our midst must either renounce Israel or suffer the consequences that they themselves have brought on—the onus is on us. The Jew brings on himself the hate that he has suffered through the millennia—a rejoinder that links the far-right anti-Semite to the far left. It is how the leader of Britain's Labour Party, Jeremy Corbyn, could call Hamas and Hezbollah "friends"; how another prominent Labour supporter, Jackie Walker, could call Jews "the chief financiers of the sugar and slave trade"; and how, in the words of a parliamentary inquiry, Corbyn, now so close to Number 10 Downing Street, could have "created what some have referred to as a 'safe space' for those with vile attitudes towards Jewish people . . . exacerbated by the Party's demonstrable incompetence at dealing with members accused of anti-Semitism." It is how a pro-Palestinian march that came just after the tragic fire at Grenfell Tower in London devolved into bullhorned chants that blamed the deaths of so many immigrants on the corporate donors to Theresa May's Conservative Party who are also Zionists. Somehow, pro-Israel sentiment in Europe caused the deadly blaze.

The renouncing of Israel thus becomes a precondition for tolerance, an insane new development in the ancient European art of anti-Semitic rejectionism. First Jews were Christ killers, then moral degenerates, then genetic inferiors. Now they're insufficiently progressive. Somehow, virulent anti-Israeli sentiment has revived the age-old chant "Death to the Jews" at demonstrations in Paris, London, and Rome. Somehow a column by a Holocaust denier, Kevin Myers, could appear in the *Sunday Times* of London about pay differentials between men and women, which included this brilliant observation: "I note that two of the best-paid presenters in the BBC—Claudia Winkleman and Vanessa Feltz, with whose, no doubt, sterling work I am tragically unacquainted—are Jewish. Good for them. Jews are not generally noted for their insistence on selling their talent for the lowest possible price, which is the most useful measure there is of inveterate, lost-with-all-hands stupidity."

But the new, European-style anti-Semitism is in one important respect very different from the anti-Semitism of right-wing nationalists, especially in the United States. The leftists who equate Zionism with racism, who demand that Jews renounce the Jewish state, are ostensibly internationalist. Their views on Israel, in their minds, comport with their broader views on human rights, the duty to marshal world opinion to confront injustice, to sympathize with the oppressed.

In the United States, the new breed of anti-Semites has an entirely different approach. The alt-right backs the Jewish state—as a destination for the Jews they long to evict from the White Homeland. (Yes, in the minds of the alt-right, Jews are not white, all appearances aside, an old racist concept regaining an airing in the Trump era.) And hey, Israelis even kill Muslims! More power to 'em. It is how, on the right, anti-Semitism and militant Zionism can coexist quite comfortably. In the viciously contested special election of 2017 to fill the House seat of my childhood neighborhood in suburban Atlanta, the Republican candidate, Karen Handel, accused her Democratic opponent, Jon Ossoff, of being at once insufficiently pro-Israel and "not one of us." Not surprisingly, Ossoff is Jewish. On Handel's Facebook page, one fan posted, "Al Franken, Jon Ossoff in Georgia, or any other ZioTalmud Khazar false-Jew needs to be screened out of American political leadership: they are of the Synagogue of Satan."

Among the threats and epithets hurled at me, someone calling himself "Rich Kayak" sent a Photoshopped picture of Donald Trump in a backhoe draining a swamp full of caricatured Jews with the question, "Time to head home to Israel Jon?" I've been told, "Go back to Israel, cuckboy"; "I hear Israel is nice this time of year"; "Scurry back to Israel, Chosenite"; and on and on. As neo-Nazis try to take the edge off their prejudice, they claim in a constant refrain that they don't hate blacks, Jews, Asians, or Latinos. They are nationalists, not racists. They believe each group belongs with its own kind in its own country. Richard Spencer, the youthful father of the alt-right, called his own movement a "sort of white Zionism." He called the white ethno-state that he envisions an

Altneuland—the old new country—the title of a utopian novel published by Theodor Herzl, the founder of actual Zionism.

Burrow down a millimeter beneath this argument, and it is easy to see that unlike European anti-Semites, their American brethren very much do hate Jews per se and do not try very hard to hide it or cloak it in academic argument. They have resurfaced all the stereotypes of Nazi iconography, which in turn was built on centuries of hate: the Jew is both shiftless, cowardly, and weak, and duplicitous, manipulative, and all-powerful. As with more ancient strains of anti-Semitism, the new breed insists that Jews are responsible for their own oppression. The alt-right is fond of asking the classic "When did you stop beating your wife" question over and over and over. "Quick question," "Darrell Lampshade" (charming, right?) asked me. "Why have Jews been kicked out of so many countries if they never did anything wrong? Please answer!"

And now that Jews have their own country, they should go there and leave the United States to the white people who valiantly claimed it long before it was cluttered by the mongrel races.

One of the memes of the alt-right is the notion that a fifth column of duplicitous Jews is constantly urging the United States on to war on Israel's behalf, that the beautiful white male fruits of true America will fight and die in the sands of the Middle East on behalf of the cowardly Jew. "We got the goyim to fight for us as usual. It's amazing how they haven't driven us back to the desert yet!" "Abraham Moshe Fuxman" once tweeted at me. "A point @jonathanweisman has no interest in acknowledging," responded "Pax Trumpiana." "He loves war as long as he's spilling goyim blood."

Israel, so it goes, should fight for itself, and the Jews orchestrating war should do so from Jerusalem and Tel Aviv, not Washington and New York.

Again, we see, national borders and walls, wherever they rise, tend to trap Jews, not liberate them.

But Jewish organizations are so invested in Israel—so committed to Israel as the central point of identification, fundraising, and recruiting—that they don't see it. The rise of the alt-right in 2016 was greeted with almost criminal indifference. Calls for unity, if not in opposing Donald Trump then in opposing the messages of exclusionary nationalism, xenophobia, and Islamophobia went nowhere. Seventy-one percent of Jewish voters supported Hillary Clinton in 2016, slightly up from the percentage who voted for Barack Obama in 2012, though down from the 78 percent who voted for Obama in 2008. Still, 71 percent is pretty high. Yet Jewish organizations—fearful of losing their nonprofit tax exemptions, or possibly angering an incoming president, or roiling the few Republican voters in their ranks—stayed silent. In truly one of the most feckless pieces of "opinion writing" I've ever read, David Harris, the chief executive officer of the American Jewish Committee, penned a column for *USA Today* at the height of the campaign turmoil and alt-right dog whistling happily recounting Ivanka Trump's conversion to Judaism and Chelsea Clinton's nuptials with Marc Mezvinsky, which included "both Christian and Jewish elements." Oh joy! he exalted. Whoever wins will bring a Jewish family to the White House!

"How American Jewish voters will respond to Donald Trump's Jewish links and pro-Israel statements—and to persistent questions about the support he is receiving from the far right, including white supremacist and anti-Semitic groups— remains to be seen. But if past is prologue, there are likely to be some Jews both loudly supporting and energetically opposing his candidacy. . . . Welcome to American presidential politics and the Jews, 2016!"

And welcome to the world of Jewish national leadership, where pro-Israel statements and white supremacy can happily coexist in a single sentence that takes no side whatsoever.

The reason for the silence wasn't only division and fear. The tribalists—the Bannonite nationalists, anti-immigration hardliners, racists, and alt-righters—included Jews: not the majority, not even many, but powerful voices who saw the rise of nationalism as a positive development for the Israeli cause. The desire to move the American embassy from Tel Aviv to Jerusalem, to renounce the two-state solution for Arab-Israeli peace talks, and to ditch the very notion of Washington as an honest broker in the Middle East trumped all other unsavory aspects of the Trump campaign. Steve Bannon knew what he was doing during the campaign when he signaled to the alt-right that Trump was their man—and signaled to the Jewish tribalists that Trump would give them everything they wanted and more on Israel. The two promises easily meshed.

In some sense, they still do. When President Trump signed an executive order ostensibly allowing churches and other religious institutions more latitude to speak out politically, many Jews saw this as a license for the Christian right to exercise its political power. The president promised a campaign to overturn federal laws that ban tax-exempt religious organizations from political speech and activities, and he extended the rights of the religious to withhold health benefits from their employees by claiming that coverage for, say, birth control violated their beliefs. In all that freedom, some saw an open door to the withholding of treatment or services from people whom conservative Christians did not particularly like.

"As the head of a religious organization, which is deeply tied to civil rights, we take real religious freedom very seriously. This order diminishes religious freedom," said Rabbi Jonah Pesner, director of the Religious Action Center for Reform Judaism.

The tribalists saw it otherwise. The Orthodox Union, still steaming over its differences with Barack Obama over Israel, couldn't resist a jab. "As a minority faith community in America, the Orthodox Jewish community depends upon robust legal protections for religious exercise. When these legal protections are weakened—as they were under the last administration—our community's freedom is weakened," the Orthodox Union's executive director for public policy, Nathan Diament, said in a statement issued after he stood in the Rose Garden and watched Trump sign the order. "Thus, we are grateful that President Trump has made it clear that his administration will promote and protect the religious liberty of Americans of all faiths wherever possible."

Rabbi Daniel Zemel, an avid reader and voluble talker from the Reform synagogue Temple Micah in Washington, D.C., told me that shul was standing room only the Shabbat after election night, and standing room only again the Friday evening of Inauguration Day. Congregants were scared, confused, and searching for answers as the New Nationalism swept to power.

Six miles away from Rabbi Zemel's synagogue, on the evening of December 14, 2016, as the new government was taking shape, the Conference of Presidents of Major American Jewish Organizations gathered for a Hanukkah party co-hosted by the Embassy of Azerbaijan at the Trump International Hotel. Azerbaijan's record of human rights abuses is beyond question. So are Azerbaijan's warm relations with Israel. The jury was still out on the incoming president's record, of course, but the views of the rank and file of Jewry were not. They had rendered judgment at the ballot box, feeble as that judgment may have proven, and they had flocked to synagogue in search of reassurance.

Though there were protests from a scattering of the conference's members, the Hanukkah party went on as scheduled, Jewish money going directly into the coffers of the Trump Organization.

"It's unfortunate that some have sought to politicize the Hanukkah gathering because of the location of the meeting at The Trump Hotel," said Andrea Levin, director of the Committee for Accuracy in Middle East Reporting in America. Morton Klein, president of the Zionist Organization of America, blasted the "far left extremists" who were objecting to the sight of the Jewish umbrella group partying in the Lincoln Library of the Trump Hotel with diplomats from Azerbaijan.

"It would have been terribly unwise for the conference to have pulled out and say 'we don't want to have this in Trump Hotel,'" Klein said. "If the Trump people became aware of this they would be offended and it would harm the Jewish organization's [ability] to have a decent relationship with the incoming president and to have access to him."

Ken Stern of the Justus and Karin Rosenberg Foundation expressed some sympathy with tax-exempt nonprofits trying hard to maintain their nonpartisan status—and their tax advantages. "The calibration is real because the lawyers will tell you there's a real risk of being perceived as taking a position in an election," he explained. "On the other hand, if there's a perceived rise of anti-Semitism and you don't say anything, why are you there?"

Rabbi Zemel had his own thoughts on what he called the final insult.

"Let's face it. The American Jewish community has been abandoned by its leaders."

THREE

The Unheard Thunder

In 2008, as an African American senator named Barack Obama was drawing huge crowds toward his campaign for the presidency, Richard Bertrand Spencer coined the term "alternative right." The toxicity of mainstream conservatism, the unpopularity of George W. Bush, the grinding futility of the wars in Iraq and Afghanistan, and the seeming collapse of capitalism at the hands of Wall Street financiers had not only energized the Left but sent the fringe Right in search of a new ideology, some synthesis of libertarianism, anti-immigrant nativism, racism, and anti-Semitism. Identitarianism had already taken root in Europe, a far-right movement marinated in racism and identity politics. But in the United States, rightist hipsters like Spencer were looking for a new new thing—one that was tied to the youthful energy of the Internet and appealed to the dispossessed of the Right.

Spencer had actually cut his teeth the year before, while a graduate student at Duke University. Three white members of Duke's lacrosse team had been accused of gang-raping a black stripper whom the players had hired for a party. The academic community was quick to condemn the privileged male aggressors, as was the credulous media that flocked to Durham and the professional umbrage-takers like Jesse Jackson, who turned the case into a spectacle. Then the stripper's story fell apart. The players were acquitted, and the grievances of white men had a new touchstone. From the fiasco, a conservative history student's alt-right star was born. Spencer delivered an angry speech at a conservative gathering at a Thai restaurant in North Carolina, blistering the Duke faculty for its rush to judgment and its propensity to assume the worst from white men. Its originality and passion caught the eye of Scott McConnell, a co-founder of the *American Conservative*, who commissioned the student to write on the case. Spencer's piece turned into a full-time job at the publication and an end to his doctoral studies.

"My life would not have taken the direction it did absent the Duke lacrosse case," Spencer later told *New York* magazine.

So-called men's rights and antifeminism have been staples of the new conservatism of angry young men, bonded through chat rooms and video games. But anti-Semitism would be the glue that adhered old-line racists with disenchanted Republicans into the semblance of a movement. In those twilight years of the Bush administration, the Jewish cast of neoconservatives who had helped plan and cheer on the war in Iraq cemented the new nativist isolationism of the alternative right. Deputy Defense Secretary Paul Wolfowitz, Pentagon war planner Douglas Feith, hawkish defense adviser Richard Perle, and conservative columnists David Frum, William Kristol, and Charles Krauthammer all had the whiff of the Other, the Jew in the backroom pulling the strings of white destruction. That dovetailed nicely with the notion of dual loyalties that has dogged Jews since long before Alfred Dreyfus was falsely accused and convicted of being a spy in France in 1894. The Iraq War allowed the dual-loyalty canard to be repackaged in contemporary garb: Jews are manipulating superior American firepower on behalf of weak but manipulative little Israel. In short, Jews are not to be trusted. Non-Jews in Bush's adventurism, from Colin Powell to Donald Rumsfeld to Dick Cheney to Bush himself, need not garner a mention.

Three years before Spencer coined the term "alt-right," a decidedly unhip William H. Regnery II, the most reclusive member of the right-wing Regnery publishing dynasty, had founded the National Policy Institute, a racist "think tank" where much of the thinking concerned the duplicity of the Jews. Regnery would use his considerable wealth to build up the National Policy Institute and the secretive Charles Martel Society, named after an eighth-century Frankish military leader who battled the invading Muslims. The most progressive members of the Charles Martel Society allow that Jews are white, but they are the outliers. "From the beginning,"

Kevin MacDonald, the brains of American neo-anti-Semitism, told a reporter from BuzzFeed, "we stressed you had to be on board about race and you have to be on board about Jewish influence."

With Regnery's money, Louis R. Andrews, a self-styled academic who peddled discredited racial theories and trafficked in anti-Semitic conspiracies, was put in charge of the National Policy Institute. Back in 1994, MacDonald, then a professor of psychology at California State University, Long Beach, published his proto-alt-right nonsense *A People That Shall Dwell Alone: Judaism as a Group Evolutionary Strategy*, followed in 1998 by *Separation and Its Discontents: Toward an Evolutionary Theory of Anti-Semitism*, positing a seemingly academic assertion that somehow Jews had harnessed evolutionary forces to develop a strong group identity—what he called a "code of amity"—while perfecting a "code of enmity" toward everyone else. Through the marvels of above-average verbal intelligence and collectivist behavior, the Jews have been adept at burrowing into the "host" culture and surviving, even if, through competition for resources, they have outlived the society they invaded. And through inbreeding and a well-honed survival instinct, Jews have become a race of their own, not white but not quite anything else, "with biological drives and behavioral patterns which come into direct conflict with the goals and values of the White race," as the ever-astute Andrew Anglin put it.

In 1999, MacDonald had something of a star turn in the high-stakes libel suit brought by the British Holocaust denier David Irving against an American professor, Deborah Lipstadt, who called him out in her book *Denying the Holocaust*. As an expert witness, MacDonald framed the case as Jewish persecution of the host. "The attacks made on David Irving by Deborah Lipstadt and Jewish organizations such as the Anti-Defamation League should be viewed in the long-term context of Jewish-gentile interactions. As indicated by the summaries of my books, my training as an evolutionist as well as the evidence compiled by historians leads me to conceptualize Judaism as self-interested groups whose interests often conflict with segments of the gentile community," he prattled on. "While anti-Semitic attitudes and behavior have undoubtedly often been colored by myths and fantasies about Jews, there is a great deal of anti-Jewish writing that reflects the reality of between-group competition exactly as expected by an evolutionist."

MacDonald, in this new alt-right world, was tasked with making anti-Semitism somehow both sophisticated and palatable—even if he was basically full of it.

In the world of alt-right sophistry, linking contemporary anti-Semitism with ancient hate solidified the intellectual argument. Thus Professor MacDonald was fond of quoting the Roman historian Tacitus: "Among themselves they are inflexibly honest and ever ready to show compassion, though they regard the rest of mankind with all the hatred of enemies."

"There is, of course, nothing 'anti-Semitic' about such a theory or its documentation," the National Policy Institute still argues. "'Anti-Semitism,' in so far as it has any meaning, can refer only to hatred of or a desire to harm Jews, and there is nothing in what MacDonald has said or written that even approaches fitting that definition. The only basis for claiming it is 'anti-Semitic' is to so broaden the meaning of the term as to include any attribution to Jews of characteristics that are not uniformly positive or to make any generalizations about them at all. For many who hurl the charge, that seems to be more than enough."

By this argument, you can say anything about any person, group, or race, and as long as it is not a direct solicitation to violence or hatred, it cannot possibly be impugned as hate speech—argument ex post facto. That's sort of like Molly Ivins's observation that in Texas, you can say anything about anyone—say, that she's a real witch—as long as you end it with "bless her heart."

This intellectual ferment among the racist right was churning largely out of view of Jewish communities battling each other over Israel and Bush and Obama and Darfur and the latest causes of the East and West Coast. Louis Andrews was running his website Stalking the Wild Taboo out of Augusta, Georgia, where the National Policy Institute took hold. Andrew Anglin, a former skinhead, founded his Daily Stormer website and mobilized his racist, anti-Semitic army out of Worthington, Ohio. When Andrews died in 2011, control of the National Policy Institute shifted to Richard Spencer, who moved operations to his home in Whitefish, Montana. The white nationalist movement was gaining steam with little notice beyond the Southern Poverty Law Center, the Anti-Defamation League, and a few other organizations and academics that specialize in hate groups. Jews seemed oblivious, despite that well-honed instinct for racial self-preservation.

Then something odd happened far afield from the standard world of hate. In 2013, a computer game developer named Brianna Wu and her company, Giant Spacekat, released a female-friendly video game called Revolution 60. A year later, in October 2014, the loutish lads in the video-game community suddenly took notice—and the alt-right found an avenue into the mainstream of the Internet.

At first, it was sheer, ugly misogyny by boys and men who must have nurtured a deep resentment toward women.

"I hope you enjoy your last moments alive on this earth. You did nothing worthwhile with your life," wrote "Deathto Brianna" on her Twitter account.

"If you have any kids, they're going to die too. I don't give a fuck. They'll grow up to be feminists anyway."

"Your mutilated corpse will be on the front page of Jezebel tomorrow and there isn't jack shit you can do about it." (Jezebel is a feminist website aimed at the Internet generation.)

Twitter trolling was born.

The threats got so virulent and so frequent that Brianna Wu and her husband moved out of their home for a time. They hired a bodyguard and a special assistant to track the threats. They were accused by their tormentors of exaggerating the threats, or even making them up. The trolls, in turn, advised each other to "incite as much butthurt as possible"—a lovely phrase that I would see over and over in my own Twitter timeline as well.

"Gamergate," which Wu was pulled into, was a heated battle between feminists and other liberal programmers who argued for more inclusive video games against the predominantly white, male gaming culture that saw the push as a declaration of culture war and an invasion of their sacred space, the "manosphere," where video-game characters could rape buxom prostitutes, mow down enemies with automatic weaponry, run over pedestrians, and pursue all manner of mayhem without judgment.

One of its targets, Zoë Quinn, mapped the leap from the narrow world of vile video gamers to the wider world of hate. First off, Quinn told me, it is something of a media-created myth that Gamergate was driven solely by misogyny.

Quinn's experience was especially gruesome. A bitter ex-boyfriend, Eron Gjoni, had compiled a bill of particulars on the video-game programmer—a mix of innuendo, kiss-and-tell, exaggerations, and falsehoods that he called "The Zoe Post"—and then published it on 4chan and a few other sites where he must have figured the loutish denizens in their parents' basements would lap it up. The horrors that followed boggle the mind. Her Wikipedia page was altered to read "Died: Oct. 14, 2014"—the date of her next public appearance. Hundreds of social media posts urged her to kill herself and pictured her covered in semen. And the threats: "If I ever see you are doing a pannel [*sic*] at an event I am going to, I will literally kill you. You are lower than shit and deserve to be hurt, maimed, killed, and finally, graced with my piss on your rotting corpse a thousand times over." Or: "We have to rape Zoe Quinn and take everything from her. We have to ruin her life."

She was "doxed"—her personal contact information posted online for a troll army ready to jump from virtual reality to plain old reality. They threatened her father, threatened her current boyfriend, and threatened her current boyfriend's new employer—in France. And that boyfriend, Alex Lifschitz, was Jewish. Very Jewish. Yeshiva educated. Anti-Semitism was part of the attack from the very beginning. At one point, Gjoni fanned the flames and held a chat with a Holocaust denier on YouTube.

"It was sold in the media as women and games because the video game industry itself has issues of gender, obviously," Zoë told me. "But honestly, the person who got hit hardest, Alex, was Jewish."

That is in large part because of what I call the Great Leap Forward. For the first week, Zoë says, the attackers were almost exclusively "nerds and gamers." Then, with her phone number having been published, a British man called her at home one morning to ask about some bogus accusation of charity fraud. She tried to make sense of his questioning, pressed him for his publication, then hung up on him when he identified himself as a writer for Breitbart News.

"Promiscuous Lying Greedy Feminists Tearing Games Apart," blared the headline above a story bylined Milo Yiannopoulos. It was September 2014, and the young, gay Londoner had joined the fray, writing a column for Breitbart that decried "an army of sociopathic feminist programmers and campaigners, abetted by achingly politically correct American tech bloggers" whom he said "are terrorising the entire community— lying, bullying and manipulating their way around the internet for profit and attention."

Anyone who has suffered through the unwanted attention of Twitter trolls will recognize the argument here: that somehow the victim of the trolling is actually the perpetrator, tormenting innocents with his or her insufferable liberalism/ Judaism/blackness. He—or, more often, she—reaps what she sows.

Yiannopoulos's intervention was crucial. Pools of hatred on the Internet already existed, in discreet websites like the neo-Nazi Stormfront. Those racists, anti-Semites, and xenophobes communed in their own world, not in the younger, hipper worlds of 4chan or Reddit or the chat rooms of YouTube. They did, however, read Breitbart.

"The whole message of Gamergate was, 'Fuck these SJWs

trying to tell us what to do,'" Quinn explained. (SJWs means "social justice warriors," a pejorative term for liberal activists.) "That jumped to Stormfront, where they were saying, 'hey, we should talk to these people, they believe what we do.' Because it was so big and visible, it was like a signal flare to a lot of different hate groups."

Within "three weeks tops," the nerds and gamers were joined by the proto-storm troopers of the alt-right in a bond that has never been broken. Hate jumped from those dedicated websites—Stormfront, the Daily Stormer, and the like—to the broader Internet, where anyone could stumble onto it. Yiannopoulos parlayed his Gamergate crusade into the permanent post of Breitbart technology editor, cementing his position as provocateur in chief of an emergent movement.

"The controversy heralded the rise of the Alt Right: a world dominated by digital trolls, insanely unbridled conspiracism, angry White-male-identity victimization culture, and ultimately, open racism, antisemitism, ethnic hatred, misogyny, and sexual/gender paranoia. A place where human decency and ethics are considered antiquarian jokes, and empathy is only an invitation to assault," wrote David Neiwert, a contributing writer for the Southern Poverty Law Center, in *Public Eye* magazine.

Social media has proven to be an ideal breeding ground and playground for Social Dominance Orientation (the belief in the inherent inequality of humans), sociopaths, and old-fashioned sadism. Acolytes of the "academic racists" who rose in the 1990s first began organizing on the Internet around the militia movements of the Bill Clinton era and the anti-immigration efforts of the 2000s. The later Bush years and beginning of the Obama era saw a shift of White Nationalist attention from liberals and LGBT-rights activists to establishment Republicans, whom it saw as insufficiently defending white rights—"cuckservatives," that bizarre conflation of "cuckold" and "conservative." The term eventually shortened to "cucks," an odd word that is at once pornographic, belligerent, and utterly meaningless. In their ever metastasizing search for enemies, alt-right aficionados naturally found the Jews and a theory that Neiwert described thus: "A small group of Jewish philosophers at Columbia University in the 1930s had devised an unorthodox form of Marxism that aimed to destroy American culture by convincing mainstream Americans that White ethnic pride is bad, sexual liberation is good, and traditional American 'family values' and Christianity are bigoted and reactionary."

The election of a black president, the Tea Party, the proliferation of alternative right-wing media and websites, the rise of Facebook and Twitter, and the proliferation of no-holds-barred social media platforms like 4chan and 8chan provided a cauldron for the stewing of racist and anti-Semitic authoritarianism. A fifteen-year-old New Yorker named Christopher Poole launched 4chan from his bedroom back in 2003. The idea was to create an open forum to post manga and anime images for obsessives of Japanese-style comic books who loved nothing more than to chat endlessly about the art form. Within days, the site was a huge success. Its secret, in part, was anonymity: you didn't need an email to register or supply any other identifying characteristic. Then Gamergate transformed it. In no time, 4chan became a trolling haven for sociopaths and sadists, neo-Nazis, racists, pornographers, and "queer-bashers." "Men's rights" activists started chat rooms that devolved into pure misogyny: exhortations to rape, feminist-bashing, and apocalyptic predictions of the annihilation of masculinity. Fifteen years later, perusing 4chan.org/pol is a frightening tour of a hate-filled underworld available to everyone, including impressionable teenagers. "Jews are parasites," writes one anonymous poster on one random day. "That being said, if they could somehow contain themselves to Israel, that would be fine. They can't, though."

A few minutes later, someone else scrawls, "I am against race mixing. Which is why I am against you being here. The jews are the problem but you are a symptom. If we destroy the jews but the country is still flooded with Mexicans whats the point?"

"So what?" my teenage daughters ask. "The only people reading these things are fourteen-year-old boys." But fourteen-year-old boys become nineteen-year-old thugs who become twenty-six-year-old website makers who become thirty-five-year-old political leaders. And anti-Semitism is increasingly in the bloodstream of our youth. Felix Arvid Ulf Kjellberg, a

Swedish YouTube superstar better known as PewDiePie, up-
loaded one of his odder videos in 2017, a silly disquisition on the
website Fiverr, where for five dollars you can pay somebody to
do, well, virtually anything they agree to: math homework, web
design, talking to Jesus, playing a computer game—whatever.
To illustrate his point, he reached out to the "Funny Guys,"
two very skinny young Indians ostensibly in a jungle who will
dance and hold up a message on the Internet. And what message did PewDiePie ask the Funny Guys to hold up? "Death
to All Jews." He played it for laughs, insisted he wasn't anti-
Semitic, apologized and apologized and apologized. But how
did he even think of this prank? What the hell? Such quips
were once overtly deemed unacceptable. In 1983, Monty Python, in their least-well-regarded movie, *The Meaning of Life*,
merrily insulted Catholics, Protestants, fat people, the rich,
the working class, and on and on—until in one scene, a
humble cleaning lady (a man in drag) says, "Though I may be
down right now, at least I don't work for Jews," an insult too
far even for Python. She had a bucket of vomit dumped on her
head for that.

It was a short hop from 4chan and the stew of the Internet
subculture to Gamergate, which targeted not only Wu and
Quinn but cultural critic Anita Sarkeesian. The owners of 4chan
announced there would be no more discussions of Gamergate
on the site. Thus 8chan was born—a whole new platform with
no restrictions whatsoever. Meanwhile, Brianna Wu had been
forced out of her house. Zoë Quinn had obtained a restrain-

ing order against her ex-boyfriend but was still being deluged with threats and hate. And the online world of hate had learned its power.

The alt-right troll army created its own vocabulary. Those complaining of mistreatment are "special snowflakes" who shouldn't be so "butthurt"; the "crybullies" want to stomp out "free speech" in their "safe spaces." The conversation spilled out of 4chan and 8chan into Reddit, the comment sections of YouTube, and then Twitter. Ironically, the trolls themselves are sensitive about these terms. Mike Cernovich—a right-wing nationalist who has denied the existence of date rape, participated in Gamergate, and promoted the PizzaGate conspiracy theory that Hillary Clinton ran a child sex ring in a popular Washington pizzeria—was horrified when the Anti-Defamation League listed him in its guide to the alt-right and alt-lite. (Leaders of the alt-lite broke from the most virulent acolytes of the alt-right in 2017 to try to soften the movement's most egregious expressions of racism and anti-Semitism, but that softening only went so far.) "The ADL is trying to get my family murdered #ADLTerror," Cernovich tweeted, to which I replied on Twitter, "special snowflake." That opened the floodgates of "butthurt" from alt-righters who claimed, alternately, that a *New York Times* editor was condoning violence and that I had audaciously and unfairly appropriated their language.

In the real world of neo-Nazis and intellectual racists, the bespectacled, aging Southerners and quasi-academics in their pleated khakis and button-down shirts gave way to a hipper set, with mops of hair and slim-cut trousers. Being presentable and appealing to searchers beyond their particular fringe has long been a problem for bigots. In the 1950s and 1960s, as bombs blew up in black churches, synagogues, and pastors' homes, and thugs in crewcuts wielded baseball bats and hurled epithets at civil rights marchers, George Lincoln Rockwell, an infamous segregationist and anti-Semite, captured the dilemma. "That's one great trouble with our movement," he confessed. "Ninety percent of the people in the movement are lunatics."

The newest manifestation of that movement faces the same limitation—but the alt-right is trying to paper it over with grooming.

"We have to look good," Richard Spencer told Salon, understanding the limited appeal of a movement of people who appeared "crazed or ugly or vicious or just stupid."

Spencer invented the term "alternative right" to differentiate his youthful anti-Semitic racism from that of the paleoconservatives who invented modern nativism, like Pat Buchanan, and the traditional right of the Republican establishment. He coined the term in 2009 writing in Taki's Magazine, a self-described libertarian webzine created by Taki Theodoracopulos, a Greek journalist who co-founded the *American Conservative* with Pat Buchanan and Scott McConnell in 2002. Less than a year later, Spencer founded his own webzine, the Alternative Right. Andrew Anglin, a skinhead troll king on 4chan, grew out his hair and started the Daily Stormer, named after Julius Streicher's weekly Nazi newspaper, *Der Stürmer*. On 4chan, 8chan, and the Daily Stormer, the white nationalists co-opted phrases and imagery from youth culture, most prominently poor Pepe the Frog, who was created by a liberal Democrat, Matt Furie, back in 2005, as part of a cast of laidback comic book characters. Back then, Pepe was most famous for peeing with his pants around his ankles. Why? "Feels good, man," the stoner frog cooed. The appearance of his fat lips, bulging eyes, and ironic smile among the new alt-righters signaled that this breed knew what was hip.

These guys were nothing like the crewcut, pot-bellied racists in the old newsreels wielding baseball bats and screaming epithets at civil rights protesters. They were self-aware, or, as David Neiwert put it, they had a trait not shared by the self-important Louis Andrews or Kevin MacDonald: irony.

When Andrew Joyce posed his "Jewish Question" on Radix Journal, the online magazine of the National Policy Institute, in 2017, the Jew he pictured was Woody Allen in the long beard, black felt hat, and *payot* he wore in *Annie Hall* as he imagined how Annie's WASP family pictured him. Now that's funny, right?

Alt-right true believers affectionately refer to themselves as "Shitlords." They extol Taylor Swift as a paragon of Aryan beauty and virtue, embrace Patriots quarterback Tom Brady as a knight of whiteness, adore the nativist character Bill the Butcher from Martin Scorsese's nineteenth-century period epic *Gangs of New York*, and pride themselves on their cultural agility. After the 2017 Super Bowl, when Tom Brady led the Patriots to a stunning come-from-behind victory over the Atlanta Falcons, alt-righters tweeted out images of the quarterback kissing his supermodel wife, Gisele Bündchen, in a pinnacle moment for white beauty and prowess. "For the white race, it's never over," Richard Spencer crowed in a February 17, 2017, tweet. Followers of the movement like to say they "red-pilled," a reference to the über-hipster action flick *The Matrix*, which featured Keanu Reeves being offered two pills: one blue, leading back to his happy but false life in a computerized virtual reality, and one red, the truth, unaltered by political correctness, social justice warriors, or cultural Marxists. Alt-righters even have a preferred musical genre, called Retrowave, which somehow evokes the 1980s, which was when most alt-righters were born.

The codes for the uninitiated can be bewildering. I thought the caricature of a big-nosed, bearded Jew—hands clasped, eyes malevolent—spoke for itself when it popped up over and over again on social media attacks—Nazi-era iconography repurposed for the Internet Age. Turns out it has a name, "Le Happy Merchant," and a whole backstory, emerging from amateur comic strips featuring a diabolical Jewish villain repeatedly taking advantage of a good-natured dullard known as "Le American Bear." The caricature "is used for the purpose of dehumanizing the Jew as a type of evil monster, rather than a human being, while also being very funny in its offensiveness," Andrew Anglin helpfully explained. Some terms have emerged online as code to avoid detection by the social media outlets they are playing on—"kikes" for example is now "Skypes." Another alt-right meme, the numeral "1488," is even more obscure, stemming from the "fourteen words" of the neo-Nazi credo—"We must secure the existence of our people and a future for white children"—and an 88-word paragraph from (an English translation of) *Mein Kampf*:

> What we must fight for is to safeguard the existence and reproduction of our race and our people, the sustenance of our children and the purity of our blood, the freedom and independence of the fatherland, so that our people may mature for the fulfillment of the mission allotted it by the creator of the universe. Every thought and every idea, every doctrine and all knowledge, must serve this purpose. And everything must be examined from this point of view and used or rejected according to its utility.

Oh, and "88" can also mean *Heil Hitler*, since "H" is the eighth letter of the alphabet.

According to Andrew Anglin, "The core concept of the movement, upon which all else is based, is that Whites are undergoing an extermination, via mass immigration into White countries which was enabled by a corrosive libel ideology of White self-hatred, and that the Jews are at the center of this agenda," as he wrote on his website in "A Normie's Guide to the Alt-Right," a "normie" being a member of the uninitiated, who thus remains "trapped in the mental-prison of the Jewish system."

"The Alt-Right is a 'mass movement' in the truest possible sense of the term, a type of mass-movement that could only exist on the internet, where everyone's voice is as loud as they are able to make it," Anglin wrote. "In the world of the internet, top-down hierarchy can only be based on the value, or perceived value, of someone's ideas. The Alt-Right is an online mob of disenfranchised and mostly anonymous, mostly young White men."

"The mob is the movement."

But their malevolence is something to behold—casual, technologically savvy, self-promotional, and absolutely vicious. In his early days, Anglin dabbled in left-wing ideology, reading Noam Chomsky and teaching English in the Philippines. "All the White people you meet are outcast sorts who you can usually connect with easily (you aren't really spending much time with Asians)," he wrote of that experience. I note this because I was a Peace Corps volunteer in the Philippines and can unequivocally say that if you want to, you can spend a lot of time with Asians, as well as with high-minded white people who are most certainly not outcasts. It is also true that the Philippines, with its sex tourism and U.S. military bases (now shuttered), attracted a lot of misfits, particularly former military men who returned to the islands after failing to reintegrate into American society. Some hook up with the prostitutes and transvestites who roam the red-light districts of Manila and Olongapo. Others, it appears, turn into racists and anti-Semites.

Anglin found his society on 4chan, then on his Daily Stormer, where he very successfully mobilized a neo-Nazi troll army that attacked not just Jews and blacks but other alt-righters with whom he disagreed. In November 2015, Anglin's "Stormers" swarmed the comments section of Breitbart with "Operation: Kikebart," incensed that the alt-right-leaning website was opening a bureau in Israel. Anglin has always been willing to police apostasy. Even Alex Jones, the unhinged right-wing conspiracy theorist who spews insanity on his InfoWars website, has felt the Anglin lash. At Andrew's urging, his trolls launched "Operation: Jew Wife," attacking Jones for having a Jewish wife. Then, in 2017, when Jones's now-ex-wife sued for full custody, Anglin's army turned sympathetic, since she was trying to "kike him." The Anglinites also mounted "Operation: Filthy Jew Bitch," targeting Labour Party MP Luciana Berger for her role in the arrest of a British neo-Nazi.

In June 2015, a disturbed young man named Dylann Roof sat through a Bible study in the basement of the Emanuel African Methodist Episcopalian Church in Charleston—often called Mother Emanuel AME Church—talking calmly with the African American churchgoers who had invited him in when he appeared at the door. Then he took out a handgun and massacred nine of Mother Emanuel's parishioners. Passages of the manifesto that Roof had written before the mass shooting matched the writings of the Daily Stormer user "AryanBlood1488"—14 words and an 88-word excerpt from *Mein Kampf.* Anglin showed no qualms. He wrote a post titled: "If Dylan [*sic*] Roof was 'AryanBlood1488,' He Hadn't Commented on the Daily Stormer in a While."

In the fall of that year, after controversial antiracism protests at the University of Missouri, Anglin launched a classic disinformation campaign to inflate the presence of white nationalists on college campuses. "Here's the plan," he wrote to his followers. "Make more of these White Student Union pages on Facebook for various universities. You don't have to go there. Make one for Dartmouth, Princeton, etc. . . . If they won't let it on Facebook, put it on tumblr or wordpress or whatever. Get it up, then forward the links to local media."

It worked. Mainstream media reports of racist student groups cropped up around the country.

In March 2016, another Daily Stormer denizen, a hacker named Andrew Auernheimer, a.k.a. "Weev," created a script that prompted networks attached to thousands of printers, many at universities, to spit out swastika-festooned fliers reading, "White man, are you sick and tired of the Jews destroying your country through mass immigration and degeneracy? Join us in the struggle for global white supremacy at the Daily Stormer." Result: another round of media stories about anti-Semitism and racism on the nation's campuses.

"Given the all-encompassing nature of the current ruling

system, our only real advantage is that we are outsiders," Anglin wrote. "When the Jewish bandit-king David killed Goliath, he did so with a dirty trick, which bypassed the established rules, thus winning a battle he could never have won fairly. The Jews did the same thing in the 60s. We are doing it now."

Andrew Alan Escher Auernheimer, who claims Jewish ancestry but counts himself now as a Mormon, boasts that he hacked into Amazon to reclassify books on gay issues as pornography. An FBI raid on his Arkansas home after an AT&T hack in 2010 yielded a pharmacopeia of cocaine, acid, ecstasy, and illicit prescription drugs, police said, but he wound up being charged on one count of conspiracy to access a computer without authorization and one count of fraud. In the techie world of hackers, all that made him something of a folk hero, earning him free legal representation, an article in *Wired*, and an "Ask Me Anything" thread on Reddit. He also did time in a minimum-security federal prison before having his conviction vacated on a technicality. But Weev got his start as a Gamergate provocateur. When I told Zoë Quinn that he had become a henchman of Anglin, she shrugged and said, "Figures."

In all of this, the questions remained: Was this alt-right cesspool dangerous? Was it growing? Or was the Internet merely giving voice to the same old cauldron of hate that had existed in the darker corners of American society (and often the bright light of center stage) since before there even was an American society?

"When I first started at the American Jewish Committee, if I wanted to see this stuff, I went to the post office box and got something in a brown wrapper," said Ken Stern, who headed the American Jewish Committee's efforts to counter anti-Semitism. "Fast forward. These groups learned how to put things online, to build an audience, then reach out electronically . . . to build a community of the like-minded."

Zoë Quinn is fed up with the dismissive talk of fourteen-year-olds in their basement. For one thing, she said, her experiences—which continue to this day, and which she has chronicled in her book *Crash Override: How Gamergate (Nearly) Destroyed My Life, and How We Can Win the Fight Against Online Hate*—were not just online. Plenty of threats were made, and invective spewed, to her face at video-game conferences and speaking events. "Most of the people who went off the hardest are grown-ass men," she told me. "The people who show up in person are not children." She has to swallow her bile when she sees prominent game developers and online personalities who joined the torturing mob take the stage at major public events like South by Southwest to promote their wares and views utterly without consequence or reproach.

"Beyond that, why should we ignore it even if they were young? Teenagers are not incapable of violence. It's asinine."

She is also convinced that the Great Leap Forward from the private quarters of Stormfront to the public chat rooms of YouTube, Reddit, and 4chan is a real threat, an avenue for proselytizing by the evangelicals of hate. "The more you hear these completely ass-backwards ridiculous notions, the more you believe them. It's repetition. Young people start out on these sites trying to be shocking. But if you joke about something, like ironically being a racist, first, it doesn't minimize the harm. Second, it's like that saying 'fake it till you make it.' That doesn't just apply to the good stuff."

That's what she calls the "radicalization effect" of the Internet. Users can circumnavigate the controls imposed by society through the curated mainstream media, educators, parents, and the like. And that can obviously be a good thing for a teenager wrestling with, say, sexuality or gender identity. But it can also be a bad thing.

"If you're facedown in a puddle, eventually you're going to breathe in some of the water."

Quinn, in her motorcycle leathers (she really does drive a motorcycle) and her colorfully dyed hair, gets backing for her views from the highest echelons of the establishment. "In a heartbeat, words can turn into violence," then–FBI director James Comey told a gathering of the Anti-Defamation League in Washington. "We have to stop the move from stewing to acting."

Two days later, Donald Trump fired him. Three weeks after that, a twenty-two-year-old follower of the "alt-Reich"—a virulent offshoot of the alt-right—came upon a young African American man waiting for an Uber near the campus of the

University of Maryland. Richard Collins III was about to graduate from college, which he had attended on an ROTC scholarship. He was a commissioned second lieutenant in the U.S. Army.

"Step left if you know what's good for you," Sean Christopher Urbanski announced. "No," Collins responded. "Step left if you know what's good for you," Urbanski repeated. Again, "No."

Urbanski, a fellow traveler on an alt-right Facebook page that mocks blacks, Jews, and women, is charged with driving a four-inch blade into Richard Collins's chest in the early morning hours of May 21, 2017. Collins was dead by the time he reached the hospital.

Five days later, a white supremacist riding the light rail in Portland, Oregon, stood in rage to castigate two teenage women, one black, one wearing a hijab. Ricky John Best, a clean-cut veteran from Republican central casting, and Taliesin Myrddin Namkai-Meche, a young man cut from a hipper mold, stood to confront the ranting Jeremy Joseph Christian. Christian is charged with slashing their throats. As he lay bleeding to death on the train floor, Namkai-Meche whispered, "I want everybody to know, I want everybody on the train to know, I love them."

Christian had different words at his arraignment: "You call it terrorism. I call it patriotism."

All of that preceded the violent clashes in Charlottesville in August 2017, which culminated in the death of thirty-two-year-old Heather Heyer after James Alex Fields Jr. allegedly sped his Dodge Challenger into a crowd of anti-hate counter-demonstrators. Two Virginia police officers also died that day, when the helicopter they were flying surveillance in crashed. The violence of Charlottesville felt like a turning point, a moment when Americans saw that we all faced a choice, that equivocation was not an option. The chanting of "Jews will not replace us," the public display of stiff-armed salutes and Klan hoods, the brandishing of phrases like "blood and soil" (an English rendering of the Nazi phrase *Blut und Boden*) have a way of concentrating the mind. And while denunciations of the alt-right poured in from politicians and celebrities, institutions and activists, the white nationalists showed no sign of even a tactical retreat. As they gathered on the Friday night of August 11 on the University of Virginia green, torches held high, a follower who goes by the nom de guerre "Bella Sassin" tweeted, "The bourgeoisie will find torchlit parades distasteful no doubt. But quietly in the soul of the nation something will stir."

Even after the violence and the condemnations, Andrew Joyce was ebullient. "It's a fine day indeed when you turn on the mainstream TV news and @DrDavidDuke and @Richard BSpencer are all over the screen raising hell," he tweeted. In a display of sociopathic viciousness, the Daily Stormer declared Heather Heyer a "fat, childless, 32-year-old slut."

William Regnery seems to have had no doubt that with his seed money, the movement is growing. In the interview with

BuzzFeed, he was ebullient. "My support has produced a much greater bang for the buck than by the brothers Koch or Soros, Inc."

In 2016, the ultimate dumb vessel stepped into the cauldron and carted the alt-right's stew of hatred into the mainstream. Donald J. Trump no doubt had no better idea of what was happening on the fringe right than the Jewish community did. He was no better versed on the chat rooms of subreddits than the Israel-obsessed leaders of the American Jewish Committee. But he was the perfect vehicle to carry the movement. From the moment he rode the escalator down in Trump Tower to announce his candidacy, he embraced the cause of white nationalism, dismissing Mexicans as rapists and criminals, declaring America's inner cities to be wastelands of carnage, crime, and depravity, and lumping all Muslims together under the umbrella of Islamist terror. Even his "grab them by the pussy" boast rang klaxons in the manosphere world of the alt-right, where lads like Mike Cernovich denied the existence of date rape and swarmed the "feminazis" who had the temerity to create video games that did not celebrate misogyny.

"I think Trump was a legitimizer," William Regnery told BuzzFeed in an exceedingly rare interview. White nationalism "went from being conversation you could hold in a bathroom, to the front parlor."

Trump wasn't the first to sow the seeds of nationalist hate

on the biggest field in American politics. Pat Buchanan's seeking of the Republican nomination for president in 1992 also stoked nationalist, exclusionist fervor and an appeal to white fears of a rising non-white majority. In fact, the folks who track hate for a living recall having feared Buchanan far more than they worried over Trump in the early days of his campaign. "Buchanan at least had a cogent way of articulating his core set of beliefs," Ken Stern recalled.

But Trump's escalator lowered him into a media environment that Buchanan could only have dreamed of—one where the Internet could play the twin roles of organizer and broadcaster, and free of charge. With that tool, the alt-right became Trump's shock troops. Anglin called for Ted Cruz's wife Heidi to be executed for high treason. (He used the charming phraseology "Mutant Ted's slut wife.") He alternately called Trump "Glorious Leader" and "Humble Philosopher," predicting, "If the Donald gets the nomination, he will almost certainly beat Hillary, as White men such as you and I [*sic*] go out and vote for the first time in our lives for the one man who actually represents our interests." After candidate Trump announced that he would ban all Muslims from entering the country, the Daily Stormer exulted: "Get all of these monkeys the hell out of our country—now! Heil Donald Trump—*THE ULTIMATE SAVIOR*." The Daily Stormer took to calling itself "The World's Most Goal-Oriented Republican Website," a motto that is supremely unfair to the Republican Party but telling of the alt-right's intentions.

When a videotape surfaced of Trump boasting to *Access Hollywood*'s Billy Bush that he regularly assaults women, kisses them whenever he wishes, and grabs their genitals, the alt-right sympathized with the attacks their man was suffering through.

"The establishment and their media enablers will maintain control over this nation through means that are very well known. Anyone who challenges their control is deemed a sexist, a racist, a xenophobe, and morally deformed," Trump huffed on the campaign trail.

Gregory Hood could not have been more understanding on Radix Journal. "Those of us who must live under the Eye of Sauron on the Alt Right felt this deep within their bones. The goal of every journalist is to destroy you. They despise you, they want to hurt you, and the hateful malice they hold within themselves must be considered every time one of these creatures is encountered," he wrote. "And the frothing, shrieking, hysterical malevolence Donald Trump has faced from the crawling chaos that is the press defies imagination."

After Trump thundered about the "Clinton machine" and its secret meetings "with international banks to plot the destruction of U.S. sovereignty in order to enrich these global financial powers," conservatives and liberals, Jews and non-Jews, smelled the whiff of anti-Semitism. In an October 13, 2016, tweet, Jonathan Greenblatt, the chief executive officer of the Anti-Defamation League, issued an appeal: "Team Trump should avoid rhetoric and tropes that historically have been used against

Jews and still spur anti-Semitism. Let's keep hate out of the campaign."

The alt-right blamed the Jews, at once saying there was nothing anti-Semitic about Trump's speech and insisting that Jewish outrage only confirmed the point Trump was making. Hood wrote: "Jewish reporters and media figures essentially outed themselves, announcing to the world that yes, they are behind globalism, outsourcing, mass immigration, and the deliberate destruction of the country. Furthermore, while they can identify themselves in this way, it is inherently anti-Semitic for others to do so."

Just days before election night, when the American media and most of the elite smugly accepted the inevitability of Hillary Clinton's victory, the heralds of the alt-right were trumpeting the coming age of Trump, when the Great Man Emperor God would usher out degenerate liberalism and launch the era of Ayn Randian noble inequality.

Another alt-right poet, Henry Olson, waxed:

Against the ubiquitous drabness and mediocrity of modern life, Donald Trump represents greatness and strength. In a time when victimhood is considered noble, Trump brags about his wealth and success. While once great and thriving cities—the Detroit of Henry Ford, the Baltimore of Mencken and Poe—degenerate into hollow husks ravaged by tribal gang warfare, we have a man who rose to wealth and fame on the dream of building the most beautiful skyscrapers in the world. While everyone around us celebrates the low, Trump Tower reaches up to touch the heavens.

On the eve of Trump's inauguration, Richard Spencer delivered a speech in Washington declaring himself and his followers to be part of the Trump movement, even as he acknowledged the shortcomings of the man he half-jokingly called the "Emperor."

"No one will honor us for losing gracefully. No one mourns the great crimes committed against us. For us, it is conquer or die. This is a unique burden for the white man, that our fate is entirely in our hands. And it is appropriate because within us, within the very blood in our veins as children of the sun lies the potential for greatness. That is the great struggle we are called to. We were not meant to live in shame and weakness and disgrace. We were not meant to beg for moral validation from some of the most despicable creatures to pollute the soil of this planet. We were meant to overcome—overcome all of it. Because that's natural for us," he said, with patented grandiosity. "Hail Trump! Hail our people! Hail victory!"

But beyond speeches and low-minded ideals, the shock troops of the alt-right had different tactics. They swarmed.

After Julia Ioffe published a profile of Melania Trump in the May 2016 issue of *GQ*, Andrew Anglin and a compadre,

Lee Rogers, of the virulently anti-Semitic site InfoStormer, were not pleased by what they saw as an unflattering portrait. They sent their troops into battle. "Please go ahead and send her a tweet and let her know what you think of her dirty kike trickery," Anglin commanded on the Daily Stormer. "Make sure to identify her as a Jew working against White interests, or send her the picture with the *Jude* star from the top of the article." He helpfully provided Ioffe's Twitter handle and a cut-and-paste anti-Semitic photo. Rogers renewed the drumbeat a few days later, exhorting his followers, "I would encourage a continued trolling effort against the evil Jewish bitch."

"Empress #MelaniaTrump Attacked by Filthy Jewish Russian Kike Julia Ioffe in GQ!" huffed "Uncle Backup" on Twitter. Another tweet superimposed Ioffe's photo on emaciated concentration camp prisoners piled into barracks. Still another photo Photoshopped her head onto the body of a Jew kneeling in an Eastern European field, a storm trooper behind her with a handgun, about to pull the trigger.

Conservative writer Bethany Mandel had the temerity to criticize Trump from the right. The response was virulent. One stalker tweeted about her nonstop for nineteen hours. Her family was threatened. Her smiling visage was pasted into a gas chamber, with a smirking Donald Trump in Nazi garb about to release the Zyklon B (an image that made its way to dozens of journalists, myself included). The charming Twitter denizen "AmeriKKKanHistoryX" sent her a photo of hundreds of Jewish corpses, her face looming above them, and another with Hitler proclaiming "Adolph's [*sic*] Oven Services: good for 6 million operations GUARANTEED." She bought herself a gun.

Julie Roginsky, a Democratic commentator on Fox News, was told on Twitter, "Keep scribbling KIKE! Americans are taking the country back from the Israel First scum. INTO THE OVEN." Attached was a cartoon of a big-nosed, bearded Jew being kicked by a jackboot into an oven with the caption: "Q: What's the difference between a Jew and a pizza? A: A pizza doesn't scream when you stuff it in the oven!"

My own experience was a little different, and a little more provocative. Once the neo-Nazis began targeting me, prompted by my tweet about the Robert Kagan column, I taunted and retweeted my harassers, hoping to publicize the anti-Semitic hate that I was only just discovering. My well-visited Twitter timeline became something of a shrine to the virulent anti-Semitism of the 2016 campaign. This didn't sit well with the S.S. command. "You've all provoked us," Anglin wrote. "You've been doing it for decades—and centuries even—and we've finally had enough. Challenge has been accepted." His buddy Weev chimed in, "Get used to it you fucking kike. You people will be made to pay for the violence and fraud you've committed against us."

But others enjoyed the exposure immensely, and to this day I'm not sure whether the publicity I provided was a good idea. When someone like me, with 58,000 Twitter followers, retweets a fascist with 400 followers, they have just performed a mitzvah for the publicity starved. No doubt I earned a lot of Nazis a lot of followers during that barrage. "Thanks to @jonathanweisman for redpilling at least 1.5k normies today by retweeting premium content. Epitome of useful idiot," responded one tormentor.

Maybe he was right.

I suppose my great service in all of this was to bring to light the three-parenthesis "echoes" that had been lurking in the alt-right corners of the web. Two journalists at the news website Mic, prompted by my writing, published a history of the symbol. It dated to a 2014 podcast called the Daily Shoah—funny, right? *Didn't exist, but boy, was it cool.* The echoes were supposed to be a visual representation of a booming voice pronouncing Jewish surnames as evil—"closed captioning for the Jew-blind," as one anti-Semite put it. "All Jewish surnames echo throughout history," explained the *Right Stuff*, the blog that hosted the podcast. "The echoes repeat the sad tale as they communicate the emotional lessons of our great white sins, imploring us to Never Forget the 6 GoRillion." In typical fashion, the inventors of the echoes also had their own obscure symbolism for each parenthetical swoosh: the inner parentheses stand for the Jewish subversion of the home and the destruction of the family through "mass-media degeneracy"; the middle parentheses represent the destruction of the nation through mass migration; and the outer parentheses stand for international Jewry and world Zionism.

But beyond symbolism, the echoes had a real function. Because search engines strip punctuation from results, the symbols cannot be easily sought out on websites and social networks. Trolls hoping to label and harass Jews can achieve their results in relative obscurity. You can't search where attacks are coming from, since the search engine won't pick up the echoes. But thanks to a Google plug-in, benignly called the Coincidence Detector, the trolls can search for you. As Mic put it, the Coincidence Detector had one purpose: "compiling and exposing the identities of Jews and others who are perceived as 'anti-white.'" A list of Jewish names, compiled by alt-right anti-Semites, were plugged into the app, which would encase those names in parentheses on the user's computer.

"With the click of a button, users are able to refresh Coincidence Detector to make sure their list of known Jews and other 'anti-whites' reflects the most recent additions to the database," Mic wrote—what the alt-right calls "belling the cat."

The app "can help you detect total coincidences about who has been involved in certain political movements and political empires," the creators wrote, using vague language to escape Google's attention. Nearly 2,500 users had downloaded it, giving it a five-star rating, before Google removed the app on June 2, 2016.

With so much publicity around the attacks, the Anti-Defamation League convened a task force to try to quantify and understand what was happening to Jewish journalists on social media. The numbers the task force compiled were staggering. Between August 2015 and July 2016, they found 2.6 million tweets with anti-Semitic language, which were seen 10 billion times ("impressions," in Twitter parlance). "That's roughly the equivalent social media exposure advertisers could expect from a $20 million Super Bowl ad—a juggernaut of bigotry we believe reinforces and normalizes anti-Semitic language and tropes on a massive scale," the ADL task force wrote in its final report. At least eight hundred journalists received anti-Semitic tweets, but they were not evenly distributed: of the 19,253 overtly anti-Semitic tweets aimed at journalists, 83 percent were sent to ten targets. I was number five on that list. Number one was Ben Shapiro, an apostate who had left Breitbart to assume a position in the vanguard of the Never Trump movement of conservatives. The alt-right blitzed him with more than 7,400 anti-Semitic tweets, a fusillade that picked up with the birth of a child during the campaign. "Into the gas chamber with all four of you," one correspondent said in response to Shapiro's birth announcement. "Globalist Dealer" fantasized about "Ron Paul grabbing Ben Shapiro by his skinny jew neck and slamming him through a table." "Who are 'the Jews' who are deliberately killing White nations? Here's one. Ben Shapiro, Jew political commentator," wrote "fin_lander," supplying a photo of Shapiro with a Nazi-era yellow *Jude* star imposed on his jacket.

The troll armies were happy to find Jews beyond the sphere of journalism. Tiny Whitefish, Montana, population roughly six thousand, looms large as the place where the virtual reality of online anti-Semitism showed its impact on corporeal reality. And no one knows this better than a real estate agent named Tanya Gersh.

The seeds of the conflict had been sown in 2013, when Richard Spencer moved the white nationalist National Policy Institute from Augusta, Georgia, to his hometown of Whitefish and, along with his mother, Sherry, bought a mixed-use property at 22 Lupfer Avenue. The top floors were to be vacation rentals for skiers in the winter, hikers and nature lovers in the summer. Businesses could occupy the street level. Although Sherry insists she bought her son out of the business, it was Richard who applied for the building permit in September 2014. By the time the National Policy Institute reached Whitefish, the area already had a vocal coterie of white supremacists. An odd little group called Pioneer Little Europe had taken root in nearby Kalispell, at the gates of Glacier National Park, in 2008, urging "racially conscious" white people to relocate to the pristine Flathead Valley. But picturesque Whitefish, on the banks of Whitefish Lake and at the edge of the national park, also attracted more liberal sorts: writers, theater types, yoga instructors, artists, actors—including Jews, maybe about fifty of them in ten households. The entire Flathead Valley, an area about three-quarters the size of New Jersey, boasts about 130 Jewish families.

Town leaders interjected themselves into the cauldron in December 2014, when the city council declared "its support of Whitefish community values that recognize and celebrate the dignity, diversity, and inclusion of all of its inhabitants and visitors . . . and protect and safeguard the right and opportunity of all persons to exercise their civil rights, including the rights of free speech, freedom of assembly, and freedom from discrimination." A local anti-hate group, Love Lives Here, tried to get the city to bar the National Policy Institute from taking up residence but settled for the proclamation. The Spencers were not to be part of that diversity. Though Sherry Spencer was clearly an integral part of the Whitefish community, the return of her prodigal son—and his rising renown—had stigmatized her. According to legal documents, the symphony board asked her to resign and returned her donation, and the Wildlife Conservancy rescinded its invitation to her to join in its advocacy. Furthermore, the documents say, the music school dissolved its advisory committee to eliminate Sherry's seat and end its Spencerite affiliation. None of that was particularly fair. It was yet another example of liberal America's reflexive response to hate: shout it down, even when, in this case, the target is a hater only by bloodline.

The tension reached a boiling point in September 2016, when the BBC aired an interview with Richard Spencer, filmed on the streets of Whitefish, with mountains and pedestrians in the background. Whitefish, in a sense, had become part of Spencer's identity as he gleefully explained how the story of America was shaped by white Europeans, how blacks could never be part of this extended white family, and how Donald Trump had energized the white nationalist movement.

Then Trump won the election, and things got much, much worse.

On November 13, 2016, as the nation was still processing

the election results, a gathering of around seventy Whitefish residents gathered to discuss the next steps. Richard Spencer had been caught on videotape in Washington denouncing the *Lügenpresse*—a Nazi-era term for "lying press"—whipping up his followers and shouting "Hail Trump!" with a stiff-armed salute. The Whitefishers proposed, then rejected, a boycott of the businesses of anyone renting property from Sherry Spencer, a pretty extreme example of collective guilt. Tanya Gersh warned friends who were renting space from Sherry Spencer that a protest of the property could be in the works and that their businesses were in the crossfire. "I reached out to the tenants because I cared about them, and I worried about them and their businesses," she told me. "My heart broke for them."

There the recollection of events diverges. Gersh's story held that Sherry Spencer called her, anguished and seeking advice. She didn't agree with her son's views on white nationalism. She regretted the grief that her property was causing the community. "What can I do?"

Tanya Gersh made a fateful suggestion. You don't need this grief, she told her. Why don't you sell the property and take some of the proceeds to make a contribution to a Whitefish anti-hate group, Love Lives Here, or maybe the Montana Human Rights Network? Sherry Spencer gave her a tentative green light, enough for Gersh to ask for—and receive—permission to charge her new client a reduced commission, one that she too would donate to the community. Gersh was ecstatic.

"Great news," she posted on her Facebook page. "Just spoke with Sherry Spencer. She is going to sell their building on Lupfer Avenue and donate some money to Human Rights Networks. She is also going to make some public statements protecting Whitefish. Building will go on the market in the next day or two. I am spear heading. Richard is moving to DC and will be done with Whitefish."

On December 12, 2016, a local news broadcast found a juicy angle: pit Sherry Spencer against Tanya Gersh in a showdown between white supremacy and liberal "New Montana." The liberal tabloid website RawStory jumped on that version the next day with a headline that blared, "Neo-Nazi Richard Spencer's Mom Faces Financial Ruin as Montana Town Turns Against Her." The story quoted Gersh as saying that Sherry Spencer "is profiting off of the people of the local community, all the while having facilitated Richard's work spreading hate by letting him live and use her home address for his organization."

Three days after the broadcast, Sherry Spencer took to the self-publishing website Medium to give her version of events— one that would put Whitefish on the nation's hate map. Under the title "Does Love Really Live Here?," she laid out her accusations against Gersh.

"Put simply, the building has nothing to do with politics— and it has everything to do with tourism and local businesses. I had no intention of selling . . . until I started receiving terrible threats in the last couple of weeks," she wrote. "These threats came from Tanya Gersh."

In Sherry Spencer's version, Gersh told her that if she didn't sell, two hundred protesters would converge on her property with the national media in tow. To ward that off, Gersh had issued a series of demands: a public denunciation of her son, the sale of her property, and a contribution to a different group, the Montana Human Rights Network. "She even shamelessly suggested that she act as my realtor! In other words, she and the local 'human rights' organizations appeared to seek financial benefit from threats of protests and reputation damage."

"Whatever you think about my son's ideas—they are, after all, ideas—in what moral universe is it right for the 'sins' of the son to be visited upon the mother?" she asked.

The alt-right answered from its own moral universe. Gersh's lawyer emphatically said the divergent versions of events are not relevant. Even if Sherry Spencer's version was right (he says it wasn't), it could not justify what followed. "There are only 6,000 Jews in the entire state of Montana, yet they're 100% of the people trying to silence Richard Spencer by harassing his mother. So Then—Let's Hit Em Up," Andrew Anglin commanded his minions on the Daily Stormer. "Are y'all ready for an old fashioned Troll Storm?"

"We are going to have a field day with you scumbags," one email to Gersh read. "If I was you I would suck the barrel of a shotgun or run to that shithole in the dsert your fkn animals stole from the Arabs. We are going to keep track of you for the rest of your life and alert any and all ppl you come into contact with of how much of a piece of shit you are."

The epithets came in a torrent: "oven-dodging Christ killer," "worthless fuckin kike," "slimy jewess." "We are going to ruin you, you Kike PoS [piece of shit] . . . You will be driven to the brink of suicide. & We will be there to take pleasure in your pain & eventual end." "This is the goylash. You remember the last goylash, don't you Tanya?" "When are you going to move your kike ass to Tel Aviv and start managing brothels there?"

They targeted Gersh's twelve-year-old son on his Twitter feed: "Ask your mommy why she hates white people so much and runs an extortion racket." A poster going by the handle "Kaiser Wilhelm II," the name of an anti-Semitic German emperor, tweeted, "psst kid, theres a free Xbox One inside this oven" over a photo of an oven.

One of Anglin's minions told her husband in an e-mail, "Put your uppity slut wife Tanya back in her cage, you rat-faced kike. Tell your scamming son to kill himself, too. Day of the rope soon for your entire family."

The threats quickly jumped the virtual-reality fishbowl. A phone call offered up only the sound of a gunshot. "We can bury you without having to touch you," another caller told her.

More than seven hundred communications—social media posts, voice mails, texts, handwritten letters, postcards, even Christmas cards (yes, really. One holiday well-wisher wrote inside a card that wished the Gershes a happy Christmas: "Dear Tanya, I realize that as a Jew your ancestors have zero traditions of free speech beyond the shtetl, but Americans [whose great-great-grandparents weren't Bolshevik Communists] would greatly appreciate if you STOPPED persecuting freedom-loving, Christian Americans, STOP BEING A JEWISH BOLSHEVIK. We know what you're doing.")—flooded the Gershes' synapses to the outside world. Tanya Gersh packed bags for herself and her family in case they had to flee.

The attack on the Gersh family was only the beginning. The day after the Medium post went public, the Daily Stormer published phone numbers, work locations, email addresses, and photographs of six Flathead County Jews, including the Gershes and their son, the rabbis Francine Roston and Alan Secher, and Rabbi Secher's activist wife, Ina Albert. Any business in Whitefish or Kalispell run by a Jew or someone with a vaguely Jewish name saw a blitz of angry reviews and poor online ratings—no small thing for an area that thrives on tourism. Transient tourists looking for a restaurant, a hotel, a bed-and-breakfast, or an outfitter would not know enough to attribute a stream of terrible Yelp reviews to a neo-Nazi cyberattack.

Richard Spencer joined former Ku Klux Klan leader David Duke on his radio show on December 26, offering Christmas cheer with a warning that "I know bad things about Tanya Gersh" and repeating the charge of extortion. Duke tweeted out Rabbi Roston's picture to his thirty-six thousand followers. On January 5, 2017, Andrew Anglin informed his followers of an armed protest in the works for Martin Luther King Day, or what he called the "James Earl Ray Day Extravaganza," a march on Whitefish that would bring together white supremacists from the United States, Britain, Sweden, and Greece. Oh, and a representative of Hamas would attend to "give a speech about the international threat of the Jews."

The next day, the president of the World Jewish Congress, Ronald Lauder, demanded that authorities block the march:

> This rally crosses the line between freedom of expression and incitement to hatred. The intention of these neo-Nazis is not just to send a political message—they are organizing a dangerous and life-threatening rally that puts all of America, including the local Jewish community, at risk. There has been an upturn of late in public expressions of anti-Semitism and hatred of the other. It is unacceptable, and unfathomable, that such incidents could happen in America.

Andrew Anglin sneered: "Currently, we have 178 skinheads being bussed in from the Bay Area on 6 large buses. Including international representatives, we will have a total of around 225 people marching through the city, though only about a third will be armed with machine guns. Others may carry baseball bats or swords, we haven't decided yet."

On January 10, Richard Spencer was back on the air with David Duke. "There was this nasty woman named Tanya Gersh who was attempting to force my mother to sell her property and to profit from it all by being her broker. It was just a really terrible situation."

"Well she's totally consistent with the Talmud and the Halacha," Duke interjected. "That's for sure."

"I'm afraid I agree with you," Spencer, the noted Talmudic scholar, assented.

That same day, the city of Whitefish denied Anglin's request for a permit, and the fearsome Nazi backed down, more self-pitying than threatening. "The Jews are a vicious, diseased race of evil monsters, and it is they who deserve to be banned as a terrorist group. Their entire existence, going back all through their recorded history, has been a series of terrorist incidents."

As she tells her story, Tanya Gersh still has to stop periodically to choke back sobs and compose herself. It was impossible to shield her family from the attacks. She had to wade through the messages in her voice mail because the threats and hatred were interspersed with legitimate calls from clients. Her most distraught emotions are saved for the treatment of her son. She tried to protect him, but she couldn't. "It's hard when your child just gets cold, to watch your child be sick. This was such an emotionally painful thing. It was painful for him."

Then, in April 2017, she sued Anglin for invasion of privacy, intentional infliction of emotional distress, and violating Montana's Anti-Intimidation Act, backed by the Southern

Poverty Law Center and a Helena lawyer, John Morrison, who had known the Gershes for twenty years.

"My ability to do my job is gone," Gersh told the *Washington Post*, since the trolling put the properties of potential clients in the crosshairs. "My sense of safety has been compromised terribly."

No one has suggested the Trump campaign had anything to do with the trolling of Tanya Gersh, but the campaign—and the candidate—did nothing to stop it. When the luxury lifestyle website DuJour brought up Julia Ioffe's treatment at the hands of the alt-right mob, Melania Trump was less than sympathetic.

"What right does the reporter have to go and dig in court in Slovenia in 1960 about my parents? They're private citizens. If they go after me, it's different. But to do that, it's a little bit nasty, it's a little bit mean," the future First Lady told interviewer Mickey Rapkin. He then asked her if, after the article was published, people put a swastika on his face, she would denounce them.

"I don't control my fans," Melania replied. "There are people out there who maybe went too far. She provoked them."

When Trump himself was asked about the anti-Semitic trolls, he told CNN's Wolf Blitzer, "You have to talk to them about it."

Blitzer pressed on gamely, but candidate Trump delivered his best profession of ignorance. "I don't know anything about that. You mean fans of mine?"

"Supposed fans of posting these very angry—but your message to these fans is?" Blitzer responded.

"I don't have a message to the fans." Trump shrugged. "A woman wrote an article that's inaccurate."

During all this, the Republican Jewish Coalition acted shamefully. I pressed and pressed for a response, until finally it released a statement that offered a master class in equivocation: "We abhor any abuse of journalists, commentators and writers, whether it be from Sanders, Clinton or Trump supporters. There is no room for any of this in any campaign."

Yes, the pro-Clinton, pro-Sanders forces were somehow thrown in with Andrew Anglin's army, apparently with a straight face.

"I don't hold black leaders responsible for some of the BLM hate I've seen, or liberal leaders responsible for the Occupy messages," Ari Fleischer, a Bush White House press secretary and prominent Jewish Republican, told me, referring to the Black Lives Matter and Occupy Wall Street movements.

Sheldon Adelson, the biggest bankroller of the Republican Jewish Coalition, and of Republicans in general, held his tongue—and quietly cut a $5 million check to fund Trump's inauguration.

"Abandon yourself to your feelings, and you must always

focus on the *Führer's* greatness, rather than on the discomfort you are feeling at the present," a former student told the linguistic scholar and German diarist Victor Klemperer in 1933.

The Trump campaign and its supporters may have wanted nothing to do with the anti-Semitic shock troops that Trump was attracting, but anti-Semites wanted everything to do with Trump. The online attacks came in distinct waves, all connected to the campaign. On February 29, 2016, as the media obsessed over Trump's refusal to disavow the endorsement of the Ku Klux Klan, a spike in anti-Semitic attacks came. On March 13, when Trump blamed Bernie Sanders for violence at a Trump rally, the neo-Nazis attacked. On May 17, when Melania Trump delivered her judgment that Ioffe had provoked the attacks on her, the minions responded again. And why not? Trump had called journalists "absolute scum."

"I would never kill them, but I do hate them," he said in the opening days of his campaign. "Some of them are such lying, disgusting people."

It also didn't escape the alt-right's notice that in 2013, Trump had tweeted, "I'm much smarter than Jonathan Leibowitz—I mean Jon Stewart"; that during the campaign he tweeted an image, generated by the alt-right, of Hillary Clinton next to a Jewish star superimposed on a background of hundred-dollar bills; that his eldest son, Donald Trump Jr., tweeted an image of Pepe the Frog with Team Trump (including such paragons of virtue as Milo Yiannopoulos, Roger Stone, and Alex Jones);

that Trump's final campaign ad inveighed against "global special interests" as the Jewish faces of Goldman Sachs chief executive Lloyd Blankfein and Fed chair Janet Yellen appeared
on the screen. Forget the dog whistles. Sound the foghorn.

It didn't end with Trump's inauguration, either. Over the
July 4 weekend of 2017, Trump tweeted a video clip from his
pre-presidential days in which the future president violently
body slammed and punched his faux-rival billionaire, WWE
magnate Vince McMahon. (Like so much in Trump's life, it
was all staged, of course.) In the updated version of the clip, a
CNN logo was cartoonishly superimposed over McMahon's
face, so the president was broadcasting to the world an image
of himself attacking the free press. An alt-right bigot who
went by the online name "HanAssholeSolo" came forward to
claim credit for this charming creation, leading others to look
back at his Reddit thread. It turned out he had also posted a
photo board of Jewish CNN executives, journalists, and personalities with Stars of David stamped in the corner of each
shot. "Something strange about CNN . . . can't quite put my
finger on it . . ." Mr. Solo mused in the latest version of
Jews controlling the media. For good measure, he also posted
a cartoonish image of a turbaned, bearded man getting kicked
in the rear by a boot labeled "We the People," with the message, "Islam, get out of America. You and your cult are not
welcome here."

Astonishingly, after a CNN reporter uncovered his identity, Mr. Solo actually took to Reddit to apologize, in part

because CNN suggested it would unmask him if he did not show contrition. He allowed that he was trying to get a rise from other Reddit users. "As time went on it became an addiction as to how far it could go with the posts that were made. This has been an extreme wake up call to always consider how others may think or feel about what is being said before clicking the submit button anywhere online that opinion is allowed. Free speech is a right that we all have, but it shouldn't be used in the manner that it was."

Such introspection, even under threat, might have given comfort to anyone who has suffered the lash of online trolling, but this was quickly washed away by the filth that followed. Picking up on the alt-right backlash against CNN, Andrew "Weev" Auernheimer took to the Daily Stormer to threaten a retaliation as vicious as the movement could muster unless the CNN sleuth, Andrew Kaczynski, was fired, his threat to HanAssholeSolo's free speech was renounced, a $50,000 scholarship for Mr. Solo was put aside (Kaczynski said Solo was actually an adult), and the network promised that "he and his family will never be harmed by your organization."

"We are going to track down your parents. We are going to track down your siblings. We are going to track down your spouses. We are going to track down your children. Because hey, that's what you guys get to do, right? We're going to see how you like it when our reporters are hunting down your children," Auernheimer threatened. He concluded, "We didn't make these rules—you did—and now we're going to force you to play by them. Hope you enjoy what is coming, you filthy rat kike bastards. Kill yourselves, kike news fakers. You deserve every single bit of what you are about to get." It was a lot of bluster, but it marked a significant moment: the troll armies of the Daily Stormer, 4chan, and Reddit, as well as the so-called alt-lite, which tends to shrink from confrontation, joined together to vow joint action.

While that tempest raged, no apology was forthcoming from the president. I'll offer Trump the benefit of the doubt and say he likely had no idea of HanAssholeSolo's past artwork. He certainly didn't know what his post would unleash. But that doesn't answer the question of why the president of the United States was swimming in the same filthy online waters as the likes of HanAssholeSolo and Andrew "Weev" Auernheimer.

In September 2017, after that episode blew over, Trump retweeted another anti-Semite who created a darling video of the president swinging a golf club and the golf ball seemingly knocking out Hillary Clinton as she boards a plane. This time, few even commented.

And let's revisit that band of deplorables I've called Team Trump. Is Steve Bannon an anti-Semite? Those who answer yes point to one major piece of evidence: his 2007 divorce proceedings, in which his ex-wife, Mary Louise Piccard, spoke of her dispute with Bannon over the Archer School for Girls, an elite private school in Los Angeles. "The biggest problem he had with Archer is the number of Jews that attend," Bannon had said, according to his estranged wife, as recorded in the court records. Divorce can be tough going, and taking one ex-spouse's word over another in court is not always wise. But that is an oddly specific accusation to be leveled by an angry ex.

What is indisputable is that Bannon turned Breitbart into a highly visible mouthpiece of the alt-right, and not just because it employed Milo Yiannopoulos. "Bill Kristol, Republican Spoiler, Renegade Jew," blared one headline, attacking the founder of the conservative *Weekly Standard* for his Never Trumpism. "Hell Hath No Fury Like a Polish, Jewish, American Elitist Scorned," a Breitbart article huffed about the *Washington Post*'s Anne Applebaum and her writings against global populism. Bannon's experience in Hollywood, especially his hyperbolic documentary *In the Face of Evil: Reagan's War in Word and Deed*, is informed by his admiration for Nazi propagandist Leni Riefenstahl. And once Bannon was finally ushered out of the White House, his reemergence at Breitbart was accompanied by a new sign, a slew of articles decrying the influence on Trump of his economic adviser, Gary Cohn, who happens to be Jewish. The name Cohn was bracketed by emojis of globes—an evocation of the "internationalist" Jew and a reminder to alt-right readers of their triple-parentheses "echoes."

Michael Flynn, the former general, Trump campaign adviser, and disgraced national security adviser, ran in alt-right circles as well, promoting the tweets of Jared Wyland, an alt-righter and anti-Semite. In July 2016, after Clinton campaign manager Robby Mook audaciously (and correctly) accused Russia of being behind the release of tens of thousands of internal emails from the Democratic National Committee, Flynn tweeted, "The corrupt Democratic machine will do and say anything to get #NeverHillary into power. This is a new low." He also shared a tweet from one "Saint Bibiana" that read, "Cnn implicated. 'The USSR is to blame!' . . . Not anymore, Jews. Not anymore."

Four months into his presidency, as scandal swirled and impeachment talk had begun, Trump tapped Milwaukee County sheriff David Clarke Jr. to be an assistant secretary for Homeland Security. Clarke's jails were under investigation for allowing four inmates to die within six months, including a newborn infant and a mentally ill man who was left to wither over seven days in solitary without water. Clarke also had ties to extremist groups and the right-wing militia movement. The Anti-Defamation League and other anti-hate groups protested mightily, to silence from the White House—until weeks later, when Clarke withdrew his name.

Then there's Sebastian Gorka, a counterterrorism adviser to Trump in his first year who publicly supported a violent, anti-Semitic paramilitary militia when he was a Hungarian political leader a decade ago. Hungary's military "is sick, and totally reflects the state of Hungarian society," Gorka explained on Hungarian television back in 2007, justifying his support for the Magyar Gárda, the racist Hungarian Guard. "This country cannot defend itself." As a twenty-eight-year-old demagogue, he signed his name "Sebestyén L. v. Gorka" to signify his sworn membership in Vitézi Rend, a far-right anti-Semitic association that is on the State Department's official watch list for immigrants presumed to be inadmissible to the United States. When all of this information burst into public, days of silence were followed by White House leaks suggesting that Gorka would soon lose his position as deputy assistant but would be sent to some other post in the administration. "Sources: Sebastian Gorka to Leave White House," CNN blared. And then he went nowhere. Just days before a right-wing white supremacist turned his car into a murder weapon in Charlottesville, Gorka took to the "fake news media" to stringently denounce any talk of right-wing terrorism. "It's this constant, 'Oh, it's the white man. It's the white supremacists. That's the problem.' No, it isn't, Maggie Haberman," he huffed, directing his ire at a *New York Times* White House reporter who happens to be Jewish.

Only after Steve Bannon had worn out his welcome was Gorka finally shown the exit at the White House—in August 2017. He had found his way into Trump's orbit from Breitbart, where he had been the website's national security affairs editor. With his patron back at Breitbart, Gorka couldn't stay. A few weeks after his dismissal, I was eating dinner with my girlfriend, Jennifer, at a small French bistro tucked away in a Washington neighborhood. At a high-top in the bar area,

Gorka and his wife sat with another couple merrily drinking bottle after bottle of red wine. It was an odd moment for me, a reminder of Erik Larson's *In the Garden of the Beasts*, when National Socialists casually mixed with the intelligentsia and elite in a still-thriving Berlin. Jennifer planned to say *Shabbat Shalom* to Gorka as he left the restaurant, but alas, we left first. He just kept drinking.

What amazes me is not how such characters can insinuate themselves into the campaign and White House of a populist conservative like Trump, but how, after evidence of anti-Semitism becomes public, Trump simply shrugs it off. As with Milo Yiannopoulos at CPAC, anti-Semitism per se just doesn't rate. You have to do something really bad, like advocate pederasty or secretly discuss the future of sanctions with the Russian ambassador and then lie about it to the FBI and Vice President Pence.

Under more normal circumstances, ugly blunders such as the one made by Sean Spicer, the Trump White House's first press secretary, when he asserted that Syrian strongman Bashar al-Assad was worse than Hitler because Hitler didn't use chemical weapons could be dismissed as incompetence, if not sheer stupidity. In a "clarification," Spicer later claimed that Hitler hadn't gassed his own people (which is untrue), as Assad did, and then brought up concentration camps, which he referred to as "Holocaust centers." The Nazis developed the nerve agent sarin that Assad used.

But it is the pile-up of such blunders that gives pause. When he met with the Republican Jewish Coalition as a candidate, Trump quipped, "Is there anybody that doesn't renegotiate deals in this room? This room negotiates them—perhaps more than any other room I've ever spoken in." The audience laughed. In the opening weeks of the Trump presidency, the White House released a statement on International Holocaust Remembrance Day that excluded all mention of Jews—an odd but insignificant omission to some but in truth the official ratification of a decades-long effort by anti-Semites to downgrade the Jewish place in the Shoah. "We are an incredibly inclusive group, and we took into account all of those who suffered," White House spokesperson Hope Hicks said.

Again, it looked like a blunder from a White House staff with an unprecedented lack of experience. When the national "Days of Remembrance of the Victims of the Holocaust," created by Congress in 1979, rolled around in April, the White House had clearly learned its lesson, dispatching the president to the United States Holocaust Memorial Museum in Washington and releasing a statement of the obvious: "The Holocaust was the state-sponsored, systematic persecution and attempted annihilation of European Jewry by the Nazi regime and its collaborators. By the end of World War II, six million Jews had been brutally slaughtered." (Never mind that the words were partially cribbed from the Holocaust Museum website.)

"This is my pledge to you: We will confront anti-Semitism," Trump said at the museum that day. "We will stamp out prejudice. We will condemn hatred. We will bear witness. And we will act."

But act they have not. As he spoke, Sebastian Gorka was still laboring away in the West Wing. And let's not forget that the State Department had prepared a Holocaust remembrance statement in January that did mention the Shoah's Jewish victims, but the White House blocked its release. Curious. Then–White House Chief of Staff Reince Priebus told NBC's *Meet the Press*, "Everyone's suffering in the Holocaust, including obviously all of the Jewish people affected and the miserable genocide that occurred is something that we consider to be extraordinarily sad and something that can never be forgotten."

Miserable genocide? Extraordinarily sad?

Trump skipped the White House Passover seder, ending a tradition that Barack Obama had observed religiously. Then, after a botched terror attack in Paris, he tried to put his thumb on the scale to elect Marine Le Pen to France's presidency and bring a once openly anti-Semitic party to the Élysée Palace. "Another terrorist attack in Paris. The people of France will not take much more of this. Will have a big effect on presidential election!" The tweet came eleven days after Le Pen said casually that the French bore no responsibility for the deportation of their Jews to Auschwitz, a historic issue long settled to the contrary. For good measure, Trump's budget proposal for 2018 sliced $3 million from the Holocaust Museum's budget. Secretary of State Rex Tillerson initially balked

at naming a special envoy to monitor and combat anti-Semitism,
saying the post was an unnecessary waste of money.

"Given continuing incidents of anti-Semitism, including over
a hundred threats to Jewish institutions in this country since
the beginning of the year, and significant incidents abroad, I
urge you" to fill the post, Senator Ben Cardin of Maryland,
a Jewish Democrat, pleaded with Trump. "Should it prove
helpful, I am happy to assist you in identifying qualified persons. I look forward to your response." It never came.

Tillerson eventually relented.

The Department of Homeland Security's $10 million grant
program to counter violent extremist ideology was narrowed
in 2017 to focus solely on Islamist extremism, not right-wing
terrorist groups, which have killed far more people in the
United States. The Trump administration also cut a $400,000
grant to a Chicago-based group that helps usher people out of
neo-Nazi organizations and the Ku Klux Klan. And who engineered that decision? Sebastian Gorka's wife, Katharine, an
advisor to the secretary of Homeland Security.

"He's going to give us space to operate, and frankly, it is
space to destroy," Mike Peinovich boasted on *Fash the Nation*,
another podcast hosted on the alt-right blog *Right Stuff*.

"Now is the time that we have to make hay while the sun
shines . . . while these investigations of 'domestic terrorist
groups' are not being funded by the government, they're not
being pushed by the Department of Homeland Security,"

chimed in "Jazzhands McFeels," an anonymous former Republican congressional staff member.

Then, in July 2017, Trump journeyed to Poland to give perhaps the most nationalist speech of his presidency. "The fundamental question of our time is whether the West has the will to survive," he said. "Do we have the confidence in our values to defend them at any cost? Do we have enough respect for our citizens to protect our borders? Do we have the desire and the courage to preserve our civilization in the face of those who would subvert and destroy it?" Lest anyone wonder who those people might be, he offered some hints. "Americans, Poles, and the nations of Europe value individual freedom and sovereignty. We must work together to confront forces, whether they come from inside or out, from the South or the East, that threaten over time to undermine these values and to erase the bonds of culture, faith, and tradition that make us who we are." The South and the East.

Amid those nationalist dog whistles, there was also a sin of omission: Trump became the first American president in decades to visit Warsaw without stopping by the monument to the Jewish Ghetto Uprising. In so doing, he handed Poland's right-wing nationalist government a victory in its own efforts to downplay the suffering of Poland's Jews while sanctifying the brave Poles in their struggle against the Nazis. This was not a mere scheduling snafu or a case of a lack of time, as the Republican Jewish Committee called it. The ghetto monument was less than a mile from the square where Trump delivered his speech. Before he had even reached Warsaw, Poland's Jewish community had admonished him. "We deeply regret that President Donald Trump, though speaking in public barely a mile away from the monument, chose to break with that laudable tradition, alongside many other ones," Poland's Jewish leaders wrote in a public letter. "We trust that this slight does not reflect the attitudes and feelings of the American people."

None of these are a big deal. But still.

A few days after the Homeland Security Department's grant decision came to light, the Mobile, Alabama, police department announced it was investigating Ku Klux Klan fliers that were cropping up around the city. They read: "TRUMP. Like it or not, he is our president. He is trying to stop illegal immigration, and the influx of Muslims [*sic*] that murder people. He is trying to lower the national debt and put Americans back to work. He has done more in the time that he has been in office than Obama did in his entire eight years in office. Start supporting your president. Join us now. Only white Christians need apply."

It was not until the bloody events in Charlottesville in August 2017 that any of this truly burst into the nation's consciousness. At a "Unite the Right" march, neo-Nazis, alt-righters, Klansmen, and fellow travelers assembled to protest the removal of a Robert E. Lee statue. Again, the chants of "You will not replace us" rang out, mixed with the clever "Jew will not replace us." Fisticuffs broke out between white nationalists and the anti-fascist Antifa forces that gathered to meet them.

The alt-right's aims were clear and articulate: leap from the Internet to the world of flesh, blood, and tears.

"For one thing, [it] means that we're showing this parasitic class of anti-white vermin that this is our country. This country was built by our forefathers. It was sustained by us. It's going to remain our country. . . . as you can see, we are stepping off the Internet in a big way," Robert "Azzmador" Ray, a feature writer for the Daily Stormer, told *Vice News* in a stunning documentary. "People realize they are not itemized individuals. They are part of a larger whole, because we have been spreading our memes, we have been organizing on the Internet, and now they're coming out."

"You ain't seen nothing yet," he added.

Blood and tears flowed. As the violence mounted, Virginia governor Terry McAuliffe declared a state of emergency and had the demonstrators disperse. Then tragedy struck, as James Alex Fields drove his Dodge Challenger into a crowd of protestors—an assault with a deadly weapon borrowed from the Islamic State handbook. President Trump was silent for hours as, one by one, Republican politicians, and even his wife, Melania, released statements condemning the hatred. Then the president of the United States mustered one of those masterly messages of equivocation, assigning no blame for the events of the day: "We ALL must be united & condemn all that hate stands for. There is no place for this kind of violence in America. Let's come together as one!"

The violence, he told reporters gathered at his golf club in

Bedminster, New Jersey, was a chronic scourge perpetrated "on many sides."

"It's been going on for a long time in our country," he lamented. "It's not Donald Trump. It's not Barack Obama."

For even many docile Republican politicians, that was too much. "Mr. President—we must call evil by its name," pleaded Senator Cory Gardner of Colorado, the ever-so-careful chairman of the National Republican Senatorial Committee, which works to elect Republicans to the Senate. "These were white supremacists and this was domestic terrorism."

More illuminating was the response from the alt-right itself, which slapped down the president that it had helped put in office. "I would recommend you take a good look in the mirror and remember it was White Americans who put you in the presidency, not radical leftists," warned David Duke, like a stern father knocking his wayward son back into line.

A day later, Trump was back in line, castigating the "very violent" Left and praising the "good people" who had gone to protest the taking down of a statue of Robert E. Lee. "Many of those people were there to protest the taking down of the statue of Robert E. Lee," the president said with ardent, almost angry understanding. "So this week, it is Robert E. Lee. I noticed that Stonewall Jackson is coming down. I wonder, is it George Washington next week? And is it Thomas Jefferson the week after? You know, you really do have to ask yourself, where does it stop?"

For that, he got a nice pat on the head from David Duke:

"Thank you President Trump for your honesty & courage to tell the truth."

Whether Trump and his family intended to, they were sending signs that are picked up like Bat-Signals by the alt-right. Even a haircut has meaning. Eric Trump's summer coif—almost shaved on the sides and long and slicked sideways on top—can make waves in white nationalist circles. When the new 'do went public, Richard Spencer quipped, "A little late to jump on the fashy-haircut bandwagon," using the oh-so-hip term for "fascism-like."

"Donald Trump got my vote the day he announced," proclaimed Jared Taylor on American Renaissance, his "race realist" webzine, just before Election Day. He predicted accurately that 60 million Americans would vote for Trump (it was nearly 63 million). "Sixty million Americans—almost all of them white—will vote for Mr. Trump, despite the most ferocious campaign of hatred ever waged against anyone in this country," he continued. "That means there are still 60 million who are not sheep. If we can reach some of those 60 million we can salvage something from the wreckage of what could have been a great nation."

Jump forward to June 25, 2017, at the foot of the Lincoln Memorial. For Washington, it was a pleasant day. Tourists wandered the grounds of the memorial, straying from the solemn slab of the Vietnam Veterans Memorial, where the names of the nation's dead of that war are inscribed, to cross over to the statues of Korean War soldiers emerging tentatively from a forest of trees on the National Mall. Between those two monuments to wars past, a few hundred acolytes of the alt-right had gathered for what they called a "free speech" rally. A Confederate flag waved beside an American one. A banner was unfurled proclaiming "No Longer Silent. We Will Be Heard. Identity Europa." A mother with a stroller scurried off when she noticed the group.

"Are we going to end up in a jail cell because a meme was just too spicy?" asked Irma Hinojosa, a Latina Trump supporter who has become ubiquitous at alt-right gatherings. "If you can't handle memes then you don't belong on social media."

"Fuck off, Nazi scum," a woman shouted at them.

"Look how ugly she is, fucking ugly," an alt-righter shouted back, reflecting the usual sophistication of the mob.

Then Richard Spencer took the microphone, looking dapper in a light tan suit, black shirt, and sunglasses. His message was more refined, perhaps over the heads of much of the gathered rabble. "There is a black cloud that hangs over whites around the world. You can call it white guilt, the legacy of slavery, the Holocaust. You can call it whatever you want," he began, before lamenting "the sense that we can't be truthful even to ourselves."

"We need to find a way out of this helplessness, and I would say the alt-right is the first step toward that."

He concluded with a peculiar pitch, one that did not use

the terms "globalist," "internationalist," "Jew," or "intellectual" but touched obliquely on the twilight fight that the tribalists are now waging.

"The greatest problem that we face, the true enemy, is a concept that was called the End of History," he said, a reference to Francis Fukuyama's 1989 essay that perhaps no one at the gathering besides Spencer had heard of, much less read. "As the Cold War ended, liberalism and Americanism lost its enemy, it lost its boogey man and it began to feel that history was over. The End of History means the end of meaning; it means there's nothing else outside of consumer products and the end of individualism." He was rambling now, referencing in his mind Fukuyama's thesis that the Cold War had ended with the triumph of capitalist liberalism and that there may not be a next chapter. Humanity's socioeconomic evolution had ended, and liberal internationalism had the last, final word. As Fukuyama wrote: "What we may be witnessing is not just the end of the Cold War, or the passing of a particular period of postwar history, but the end of history as such: that is, the end point of mankind's ideological evolution and the universalization of Western liberal democracy as the final form of human government." In Fukuyama's treatise, Richard Spencer found the idea that had to be beaten, that the alt-right had been born—or reborn—to clear the path for a new ideology to restart history, white nationalism, a cause that would crush soft-headed liberalism. "Our greatest enemies will tell you there's nothing more to fight for, that it's over," he shouted in a strange intellectual crescendo. "We are going to fight for a future! We are going to start history all over again!"

The crowd chanted "Hail Victory!" and "You will not replace us!"

The Jews slept.

FOUR

Stand Up or Ignore

David Bernstein, a conservative law professor at George Mason University, thinks he knows why so many Jews are alarmed at the rise of anti-Semitism in the era of Trump: they don't like him.

Jewish discomfort is unquestionable. In an article in the *Washington Post*, Bernstein quoted Andrew Silow-Carroll, editor in chief of the Jewish Telegraphic Agency:

Most Jews didn't vote for him, and regarded his campaign antics as particularly unsettling, from his appeal among white supremacists and ethno-nationalists to his willingness to exploit the country's racial and ethnic divides. In his embrace of a fiercely chauvinistic "economic nationalism," White House strategist Steve Bannon represents something "unprecedented and inconceivable" in the minds of many Jews. Until Trump, resurgent nationalism seemed a problem for Europe, where economic malaise, fear of immigrants and the ghosts of the 20th century have combined into a particularly toxic brew on the right.

But does that add up to the greatest upswell of actual anti-Semitism that we have seen since the 1930s? Bernstein pointed to a *Wall Street Journal* story from 1995 that fretted,

> These are anxious times for American Jews. Still reeling from the results of the November election, many liberal Jews are alarmed by the rise of the religious right. They are increasingly uncomfortable with verbal attacks by conservative commentators on the "cultural elite" and on "Hollywood," both of which they believe are code words for Jews. And they are shaken by well-publicized reports of neo-Nazi groups and of anti-Semitic violence by teenage "skinheads."

But those earlier fears proved to be groundless. With the benefit of hindsight, the Republican "revolution" that swept Newt Gingrich to power in the House did not herald an era of uncertainty for Jews. It cemented the power of Israel in American foreign policy; ushered in the "Jewpublican," who strengthened the Jewish position in society by divorcing Judaism from a single party; and eventually gave us Eric Cantor, the first Jewish House majority leader.

And measuring this anti-Semitic surge is just plain difficult. Before it devolved into a deadly melee, the "Unite the Right" rally in Charlottesville in August 2017 was likely the largest gathering of white supremacists in more than a decade. Images of Nazi salutes, swastika flags, and angry white men chanting "Jew will not replace us" leave an indelible imprint, and the numbers back up the fear. The Anti-Defamation League trumpeted a 34 percent increase in assaults, vandalism, and harassment in 2016 over 2015, with 1,266 total acts targeting Jews and Jewish institutions, nearly 30 percent of them coming in November and December, after Donald Trump's unlikely election triumph. More troubling, the surge powered into 2017, with another 541 incidents by the early summer, putting 2017 on pace to top two thousand incidents. The first three months of 2017 saw 161 bomb threats and 155 acts of vandalism, including three cemetery desecrations. In Denver, vandals scrawled "Kill the Jews, Vote Trump." In St. Petersburg, Florida, a Jew was accosted by an assailant shouting "Trump is going to finish what Hitler started."

"These incidents need to be seen in the context of a general resurgence of white supremacist activity in the United States," said Oren Segal, who directs the Anti-Defamation League's Center on Extremism. "Extremists and anti-Semites feel emboldened and are using technology in new ways to spread their hatred and to impact the Jewish community on and off line."

True, no doubt, but look a little deeper at the ADL's numbers. Nearly half the harassment incidents catalogued in the

first three months of 2017 were bomb threats, and the bulk of
those came from a teenage Jew in Israel with a brain tumor
and a mentally unbalanced former journalist trying to get
even with an ex-girlfriend. The ADL's Jonathan Greenblatt was
quick to say that those bomb threats, regardless of the prove-
nance, were still anti-Semitic acts. If so, they were acts with an
asterisk. The number of physical assaults over that time, six, represented a decline of 40 percent from the first quarter of 2016.
And the thirty-six anti-Semitic physical assaults recorded in
2016 represented a 35 percent decline from 2015. As the alt-
right loves to say, the Anti-Defamation League makes its money
off sounding the siren of anti-Semitism. Or as the alt-right minions actually say, with their inimitable eloquence, "Anudda
shoah, muh 6 gorillion."

The fact is, the threat of violence against Jews has not ma-
terialized into actual violence aimed specifically at us. On each
end of the North American continent, within days of each
other, alt-right thugs knifed and killed an African American
on the verge of his college graduation in Maryland and two
white men in Portland who stood to defend an African American and a Muslim teenager on the light rail. Weeks later, in a
rage, a white supremacist in Charlottesville mowed down
counterprotesters with his car, killing one and injuring twenty.
But so far, nothing like that has been aimed at Jews per se.
A somewhat peculiar 2017 Pew Research Center poll decided
that Americans view Jews more warmly than they do any
other religious group, with Catholics at our heels. "Americans

express warm feelings toward Jews, with half of U.S. adults rating them at 67 degrees or higher on the 0-to-100 scale. Four-in-ten Americans rate Jews in the middle of the thermometer, between 34 and 66, and only about one-in-ten express feelings that fall at 33 degrees or cooler."

Since 1964, the Anti-Defamation League has kept tabs on American attitudes toward Jews with polling every few years that lays out various stereotypes: the Jews have too much power in business, the Jews control Wall Street and the media, and so on. In 1964, the ADL concluded, 29 percent of Americans harbored some anti-Semitic beliefs. In 2016, the latest checkup, 14 percent did—about two percentage points higher than 2013 but well within the poll's margin of error. Steady as she goes.

"The number of Americans that hold anti-Semitic beliefs has decreased dramatically," Greenblatt told me. "We feel very good about that."

Yet Greenblatt and others really worry about the ability of the alt-right's form of hate to metastasize in an American society where the norms of decency and tolerance are fraying and the president of the United States is seen not as a bulwark against hate but, at the very least, as tolerant of it. After Jeremy Joseph Christian allegedly slashed the throats of Ricky John Best and Taliesin Myrddin Namkai-Meche in Portland, the nation waited for President Trump to speak out, at least on his beloved Twitter. We waited and waited. The day after the stabbing, on May 28, 2017, the president boasted, "Big win in Montana for Republicans!," praising the victory in a

House special election of a candidate, Greg Gianforte, who, the night before Election Day, had choked, picked up, and body-slammed a reporter for the *Guardian*. Trump decried "fake news" and tweeted about tax cuts, health-care legislation, and a North Korean missile launch. Finally, after pleading from anti-hate activists, on May 29, this message appeared on his official @POTUS account, the one he doesn't run and doesn't really care about: "The violent attacks in Portland on Friday are unacceptable. The victims were standing up to hate and intolerance. Our prayers are w/ them." He never made any comment on his @RealDonaldTrump account, the one that Americans watch with fascination and fear. I'm quite sure that was not lost on the alt-right.

Trump equivocated on Charlottesville in the most flagrant way possible, at first decrying violence on all sides, then having his White House release a stronger statement unattached to his name, and then, three days after Heather Heyer's death, finally speaking out. "Racism is evil. And those who cause violence in its name are criminals and thugs, including the KKK, neo-Nazis, white supremacists, and other hate groups that are repugnant to everything we hold dear as Americans." After a bipartisan chorus looked askance at a statement that looked like a hostage video, the president reverted back to his time-honored victimology. "Made additional remarks on Charlottesville and realize once again that the #Fake News Media will never be satisfied . . . truly bad people!" he wailed on Twitter.

It is social media that has so many hate-crime experts worried. "What we're seeing today is not an increase in anti-Semitism," Greenblatt says,

> But it is important. What is profound is that social media is creating a public conversation that we have not seen in many, many, many years. With the Internet, in all its complexity, variety, and technology, from bulletin boards to websites, the haters cannot just find one another but can connect effectively. Something is different. When Father Coughlin was on the radio, people could listen to it, but presidential candidates didn't pick the language up. Now, something on 8chan or some weird thread posts on Reddit leaps onto InfoWars, then the Washington Free Beacon, and on to Fox News and the Twitter feed of a presidential candidate or the president. You are seeing it spread and infiltrate, and we as Jews know what happens when weird ideas get weaponized.

Zoë Quinn, who at thirty is a true child of the World Wide Web, put it this way: "I'm weirdly lucky to have grown up with the Internet when I can remember a time without it. It feels like this old friend from high school who's really smart about some things but is also fucking embarrassing. There used to be a joke in the nineties: 'Hey, it must be true, I read it on the Internet.' That was a joke because we knew it was bullshit. Well, not anymore."

It is not a foregone conclusion that the views of a small minority can affect the mainstream, but there's plenty to worry about. Yes, the Gingrich revolutionaries were not anti-Semites, but the anger that swept them into office and the virulent contempt for Bill Clinton in those years planted the seeds of Ruby Ridge and Waco, Oklahoma City and the "Justus Township" of the Montana Freemen. These were scarring events. In August 1992 at Ruby Ridge, near Naples, Idaho, U.S. marshals confronted an apocalyptic survivalist named Randy Weaver who had been on a government watchlist for years. The shootout that followed took the lives of a deputy U.S. marshal, William Francis Degan; Weaver's fourteen-year-old son, Sammy; and a Weaver family dog. During the eleven-day siege that followed, an FBI sniper killed Randy Weaver's wife, Vicki. Finally, on August 30, Randy Weaver and his surviving children surrendered, the dead now martyrs to the anti-government cause. The next year, between February 28 and April 19, federal agents laid a far more consequential siege to another apocalyptic group that was armed to the teeth, the Branch Davidians. When fire finally engulfed David Koresh's compound outside of Waco, Texas, seventy-six followers—men, women, and children—were incinerated. Two years later to the day, Timothy McVeigh and Terry Nichols pulled their rented Ryder truck in front of the Alfred P. Murrah Federal Building in Oklahoma City and detonated 4,800 pounds of ammonium nitrate, nitromethane, and diesel fuel, leveling the building, killing 168, and wounding more than 680. In between and after were any number of standoffs between federal authorities and right-wing militias, from the Montana Freemen in "Justus Township" to Cliven Bundy in Bunkerville, Nevada, to the seizure of the Malheur National Wildlife Refuge in Harney County, Oregon.

The hatred of government that spawned the militia movement in the 1990s sparked the vigilante Minutemen a few years later and then the Tea Party, the Freedom Caucus, and the alt-right. And now there is Donald Trump.

In May 2017, the august National Bureau of Economic Research issued a peer-reviewed paper titled "From Extreme to Mainstream: How Social Norms Unravel," by Leonardo Bursztyn of the economics department at the University of Chicago, Georgy Egorov of the Kellogg School of Management at Northwestern, and Stefano Fiorin of the UCLA Anderson School of Management. It raised an odd question for an academic paper: could entrenched social norms unravel quickly? To answer it, they examined xenophobia and the Trump campaign. To begin, they posited that "even individuals with very strongly-held political views might avoid publicly expressing them if they believe their opinion is not popular in their social environment." They then set out to examine what could change that. And what could change that, they concluded, was an election where societal views that were kept under wraps were suddenly and widely exposed.

"If most individuals assume that a specific opinion is stigmatized, the stigma might be sustained in equilibrium," they wrote. But "Donald Trump's rise in popularity and eventual victory during the 2016 U.S. presidential campaign causally increased individuals' perception of the social acceptability of holding strong anti-immigration (or xenophobic) views and their willingness to publicly express them."

To test their hypothesis, subjects were told that they would be given the chance to donate some of their research payment to a randomly drawn organization that could either be pro-immigration or anti-immigration. Unbeknown to them, more than 90 percent of the subjects were offered one group: the Federation for American Immigration Reform, which is decidedly against immigration. FAIR's views were made very clear—it was described as an "immigration-reduction organization." Before the unexpected triumph of Donald Trump, people were much more likely to reject contributing to FAIR if that contribution was publicly acknowledged than if it was kept hush-hush, suggesting that such a contribution carried a shame factor. But in states where Trump was clearly popular and surging, the giving rates between anonymous and public donors disappeared, along with the stigma. And after the election, when the popularity of Trump's views was publicly ratified, donation rates soared.

The writers concluded: "Our framework thus illustrates how a shock to the information possessed by individuals, such as an election where this particular issue (tolerance vs. xenophobia) is salient, can rapidly change the social norm in communication behavior: what was unacceptable and rarely, if ever, spoken, could become acceptable and normal in a matter of weeks, if not days." Compounding this frightening conclusion was its corollary: "Information aggregation can make an 'extreme' topic 'mainstream,' but not the other way around: such a shock cannot make a mainstream topic extreme. This is easy to see: if a topic is mainstream and socially acceptable, individuals know how widely and by whom each opinion is shared, in which case information aggregation is unlikely to reveal new information."

In other words, a social genie can escape its bottle fast, and that genie can't be shoved back in. Societies can change for the worse, and we are not destined for inexorable progress. I am always reluctant to say this, but here it can't be avoided: witness Germany, 1933.

David Saperstein, a prominent and outspoken Reform rabbi, lawyer, and ambassador who was once called "Obama's Rabbi," was blunt: The president is "koshering" racism with his politics.

"This feels like a different moment," he told me as we walked through the Washington, D.C., neighborhood of Dupont Circle to a deli run by Koreans from his office at the Religious Action Center of Reform Judaism. "There are dynamics we've never seen before, they're all coming together, and if we don't act to preserve the concepts of diversity, inclusion, of *E Pluribus Unum*, if we don't restore those norms, the America that we know might not be there for our children."

That sentiment isn't just shared in liberal Jewish circles,

alarmist anti-hate groups, and academia. After the Gianforte body-slamming incident, Representative Mark Sanford,
a conservative Republican from South Carolina, noted in a
tweet, "There is total weirdness out there. And like I said,
he's unearthed some demons, and people feel like if the president of the United States can say anything to anybody at
any time, then I guess I can too, and that is a very, very dangerous phenomenon." Those sentiments came from a man
who, as governor of the Palmetto State, achieved fame by
claiming to be hiking the Appalachian Trail as he was pursuing a clandestine affair in Argentina. He knows what's
weird. (Gianforte easily won the election, then pleaded
guilty to misdemeanor assault charges and took his seat in
Congress.)

Ignoring those dynamics won't make them go away.

As Zoë Quinn put it in her inimitable way, "The thing that
really gets me is this notion that any response emboldens them.
No, what emboldens them is showing that there are no consequences for behaving like fucking little monsters."

But what does confronting them do?

John Morrison, the Montana lawyer who is representing
Tanya Gersh against Andrew Anglin, has no doubts. "In Montana we have a problem with noxious weeds. When they pop
up, you pull them up by the roots. The worst thing you can do
is allow them to spread," he told me. Yes, the assault that Anglin's trolls visited upon Tanya Gersh never graduated to physical violence, but it was violent intimidation nonetheless,

unsettling the family, destroying their businesses, driving them into therapy, and turning their lives upside down. The complaint filed against Anglin describes very physical results: panic attacks, nightly sobbing, weight gain, hair loss, bursitis, hip and shoulder pain. "Ms. Gersh has sought and received medical care to relieve the symptoms of her distress. Her primary care physician has, for the first time, prescribed antidepressants, valium, and acupuncture. She has also started to going to trauma therapy twice a week."

"This is not some sort of protest lawsuit," he said, speaking with the slow cadence of a man choosing his words carefully. "This is a reaction to actual harm inflicted. It's simply unreasonable to expect victims to laugh it off or walk away."

Of course, battle plans rarely survive contact with the enemy. Lawyers for the Southern Poverty Law Center have had a devilish time just trying to find Anglin to serve him his papers.

Whitefish illustrates the dilemma of Jews in the time of Trump. To some, the lesson of Whitefish is clear: ignore the bullies and they will slink back to their caves. My own rabbi, Sunny Schnitzer, at Bethesda Jewish Congregation in suburban Washington, reached that conclusion. Attention, he said, is the oxygen that the likes of Andrew Anglin need in order to thrive. Rabbi Sunny would certainly not dismiss Tanya Gersh as an acceptable casualty in his war of passive resistance. Gersh's victimization is tragic. But the outcome of the non-showdown is what matters and, from the outside, the Jews of Whitefish appear to have emerged from the confrontation stronger, more cohesive, and more secure in their community. Even Tanya Gersh speaks of the support she received from all over the nation, even the world, but especially from Whitefish, where residents placed menorahs in their windows, showered her with love letters, and encircled her family with protection and well-wishes.

"We have security at all of our events now because there is a constant state of fear," Gersh says of the Jewish community. "It's a huge financial burden, but it brought us together. It definitely brought us together. I love my little town, and my community stood up for me one hundred percent of the time."

Mission accomplished—sort of.

The reality is far more complicated. I spoke with Rabbi Francine Green Roston, whose diffuse congregation, the Glacier Jewish Community, covers hundreds of miles of northwest Montana. A transplant from New Jersey, Rabbi Roston holds Shabbat services once a month in her Whitefish home. Religious holidays are celebrated in local hotels. And the Jewish community of the Flathead Valley is not quite as united as advertised. Some of the old-timers believe that Tanya Gersh violated a cardinal rule when she inserted herself into the Spencers' affairs, that Rabbi Roston shouldn't have talked to the press, that Ina Albert should have kept her name out of the press, that Jews in Montana should keep their heads down and their voices low and mind their own business. They believe that some of the newer members of the community are social justice warriors who were itching for a fight and welcomed the attention of the Anti-Defamation League, the Southern Poverty Law Center, and the Secure Community Alert Network security professional who drove through the night from Seattle to help the Jews of Whitefish defend themselves, as well as the myriad synagogues, churches, and anti-hate organizations that were prepared to converge on their tiny town for a showdown with the neo-Nazis.

The fact is, there was another way besides fight, flight, or freeze, what Rabbi Roston equates to a boxing match: absorb the blows, duck the punches, preserve your energy, and fight back at the right time, after your opponent begins to tire. The threats to her congregants, to her community, to herself, and to her family were very real. Yes, most of the phone calls, emails, and social media posts were from around the country, even around the world, but Montana is Montana: white supremacists were nearby, and guns were everywhere. At one point, the calls online to target Whitefish businesses were so specific and so accurate that it became clear they were coming from within the community itself. A little online sleuthing and Roston realized that another parent in her children's school was supplying targets to the Daily Stormer. Roston recalled a night during the confrontation when she broke down in tears with a friend, frustrated that she couldn't speak out. But she said she had to remember the immediate imperative.

"My instinct was to speak out, but when your children's safety is at risk, it doesn't matter how strong my calling is to *tikkun olam*, to fix the world. I had to protect my kids."

So all those supportive offers from well-meaning groups and individuals hoping to come to Whitefish to confront the neo-Nazis were politely declined. Reporters' inquiries went unanswered. Ron Lauder's appeal from the World Jewish Congress wasn't greeted with cheers but with dismay, as the alt-right tried to use it as proof that the International Jewish Conspiracy was rallying to the defense of little Whitefish. The Jews of Whitefish wanted to be left in peace.

The threat, though quieter now, is not gone. A community that once bragged of never locking its doors and leaving car keys in the ignition now posts armed guards at all Jewish events. But when the Southern Poverty Law Center approached Gersh in April 2017 about suing, she didn't hesitate. For many, many months, she said, she was silent. "We were just trying to heal and take in what had happened." But presented with the chance to strike back, she realized silence wasn't enough. "I think that once I understood that he had done this to other people, I realized I couldn't live with myself if I didn't have some part of trying to stop it."

Richard Cohen, the president of the Southern Poverty Law Center, saw in the Gershes' trial an opening to do serious harm to Andrew Anglin and the Daily Stormer. The Alabama-based anti-hate organization had filed lawsuits against hate-group leaders in the past, seeking to hold them responsible for the violent actions of their followers. With the Whitefish saga, the SPLC had "an opportunity to apply familiar principles in a new context," he explained to me—an anti-hate action for the digital age. The goal is simply to put Anglin out of business by winning as large a judgment as possible and then pursue it for the twenty years that the statute allows. "I don't know what kind of assets Mr. Anglin has, but one of the things we can do is make him pay a price for what he has done," Cohen said.

Cohen acknowledged that Anglin loves the attention. He immediately began fund-raising off the lawsuit. "Anglin's being sued by the SPLC for lawful, First Amendment–protected criticism of Jewry. The site needs a huge chunk of cash to keep going. Right now," the Daily Stormer pleaded. Accompanying the appeal was a picture of Anglin's and Gersh's faces Photoshopped on Gustave Moreau's painting "St. George and the Dragon," showing Anglin as St. George piercing Gersh as the dragon. "In order to survive we need shekels." An online fund-raising tool set a $150,000 minimum, and by early June that goal had been exceeded. Sam Hyde, the alt-right's favorite comedian, contributed $5,000. When he was reached for comment by a *Los Angeles Times* reporter, Hyde asked if the reporter was Jewish.

Tamer circles of the alt-right rallied around Anglin as well, claiming that while they could not countenance all of the Daily Stormer's foul language and rhetoric, they could not tolerate the Southern Poverty Law Center's flagrant attempt to silence free speech. "That the SPLC, of all organizations, should be pressing forward on such grounds is ironic to say the very least. Aside from scare-mongering among old, wealthy Jews in order to solicit donations and bequests, the SPLC's entire *modus operandi* has for some time revolved around 'exposés' of Nationalist figures. Although these doxings are dressed up as 'Intelligence Reports' forming part of an overall 'Hatewatch' strategy, in reality they are little more than grubby, sensationalized, and often libelous attempts at political intimidation," huffed Andrew Joyce, Ph.D., in the Occidental Observer, Kevin MacDonald's online magazine of "White Identity, Interests, and Culture." (The alt-right is masterful at the "I know you are, but what am I?" strategy of accusing its opponents of employing tactics that it uses, like doxing and online intimidation.)

Joyce, an inveterate anti-Semite masquerading as a scholar, begins his defense of Anglin with an oft-quoted trope: "The Jew cries out in pain as he strikes you."

To Cohen, those responses do not outweigh the imperative of striking back. "You have a choice when you encounter a bully. You can be quiet and hope he goes away or chooses a different target next time, or you can fight," he said, adding, "This is not a matter where someone could just avert one's eyes."

The Jewish response to the alt-right has been an argument over tactics: Which action can best counter the rising presence of this new anti-Semitism? But in some sense this again reveals the strange, ungrounded nature of American Jewry.

Daniel G. Zemel, the thoughtful, sometimes flummoxed rabbi of Temple Micah in Washington, D.C., refers to himself as "a simple synagogue rabbi." He proposed another reason that Jews must respond: moral imperative. Religious Christians would respond unapologetically to this question with a one-word answer: Scripture. This really isn't a choice: the Jew is obligated to counter injustice.

"I don't go looking to pick fights, but a central Jewish lesson is to oppose evil in all forms," Rabbi Zemel told me.

Jews don't cower; we hope. Because we believe the Messiah has yet to come, we do not look back at any Golden Age. We look forward with anticipation, and we fight for our future. As the Modern Orthodox rabbi Yosie Levine wrote last year, ruminating on rising anti-Semitism and the approaching Passover, "To be a Jew is to be a beacon of hope in a world perpetually threatened by the pall of despair. The whole trajectory of the Seder leads us to the final cup of universal redemption. It impels us to see the world through the prism of what it ought to look like, but does not yet."

That this struck me as revelatory is a painful indictment of my own thinking and a telling moment for my thinking about the Jewish community at this point in American history. I had been struggling with my own views on how to confront the alt-right when I agreed to meet Rabbi Zemel for lunch at the DC Boathouse, in what is known as "Upper Caucasia," the very white quadrant of the District near the border of Bethesda,

STAND UP OR IGNORE

Maryland. A larger context—morality, the never-simple but always-important question of what is right—had not even entered my mind during this struggle. Like so many American Jews today, for me the embrace of theology does not come naturally. Zemel took no time landing on it. The moral response is imperative. Morality can inform tactics. We should certainly consider what response would be most effective: marches, vigils, lawsuits, street brawls, studied indifference. But the tactics we employ should be grounded in a principle, a belief, a morality. And American Jewry is simply not grounded at the moment.

He raised the Talmudic adage on the Torah: "Turn it, and turn it, for everything is in it. Reflect on it and grow old and gray with it. Don't turn from it, for nothing is better than it."

All of this invocation of scripture is not to say that, as fundamentalist Christians believe, the Bible is all truth and diktat. No, the Torah holds everything: goodness and cruelty, right and wrong, brilliance and folly, wisdom and foolishness. We should turn to it because the answers are there to be found, but we must search for them.

Zemel's sermon on Rosh Hashanah was clear-eyed and unflinching as he lamented the pall cast over the nation by our new president. But he was as instructive to the Jews in the congregation as he was critical of the man in the White House. Judaism is at heart pluralistic, a religion and a culture always open to another voice, D'Var Recher. But all of those voices in the public sphere must form a chorus of "we." If those shouting are only shouting for themselves, "that way is the way toward Sodom and Gomorrah."

Judaism, or at least Reform Judaism and much of Conservative Judaism, is stuck in what the French philosopher Paul Ricoeur calls the Critical Distance phase of spiritual development. The first phase, the First Naïveté, is the acceptance of the myths that our ancestors developed to explain what they could not understand—the literal belief in the word of the Torah or the Bible or the Koran or any number of other religious texts. It is fundamentalism: unchanging, unquestioning, and grounded in the literal words attributed to our God or gods. But the Enlightenment and the development of the scientific method pulled us back from those myths and gave us a vantage point from which they made little sense. The questions can be simple: When Adam and Eve were thrown out of the Garden of Eden, Cain slaughtered Abel and was left to wander the world with the mark of Cain upon him. Who was out there to encounter that mark? With whom did he mate to produce the species we call humanity? They can be more searching: How the hell can we believe in a God that sent she-bears to rip children apart just because they taunted his servant Elisha with the equivalent of "baldy, baldy, baldy"—"Up with thee, bald head." Rationality is a vexing force for spirituality, and this Critical Distance has doused the spark of religion in many generations—and in many Jews.

But Ricoeur posits a third phase after the stage of enlightenment, what he called the Second Naïveté, a phase in which we accept the myths as myths but examine them as metaphor, open our minds to their interpretations, and see the stories as something greater than their literal meaning. They call to us to develop our own personal interpretations and private spirituality—our own moral grounding. "Beyond the desert of criticism, we wish to be called again," Ricoeur writes.

Rabbis are expert at calling their congregants to the Second Naïveté, at seeing what they perceive to be a hidden and powerful need for moral grounding. But Jewish institutions are terrible at embracing it. It's as if Jewish leaders fear that an open discussion of scriptural morality would make Jews vulnerable to the judgment of religions far more practiced in straightforward judgment, or that we would be reduced to the level of rank moralism. Too many of us see ourselves as above the intellectual level of conservative Christians and Muslims, yet we also feel threatened by them. Jews love nothing more than to argue, so our organizations and leaders give us the Battle for Israel's Survival like a modern Jewish bread and circus, while the lawyers argue over tactics. Even in synagogue, what passes for an upswell of spirituality is really a dependence on the mechanics of religiosity. Where Christians delve into the depths of spiritual meaning, we just add more Hebrew. What feels like religion is really just an added layer of tradition.

When I was bar mitzvahed in 1978, I learned a Torah portion in Hebrew as well as the prayers before and after the

Torah reading—and that was it. I delivered my *d'var Torah*, my sermonette, in English, with no *haftarah*, no singing of the *kiddush* or leading of other prayers. After my divorce, my younger daughter, Alissa, wanted nothing more than to be bat mitzvahed, and we joined a congregation that was perhaps the most liberal Reform synagogue in the area—out of convenience (it was close to home) and because Alissa had a close friend with whom I hoped to strike up a carpool relationship. But even at Bethesda Jewish Congregation, ensconced in the building of Bradley Hills Presbyterian Church, Alissa learned far more Hebrew, conducted a far more involved service, chanted a lengthy Torah portion and *haftarah* portion, and now knows far more of the Hebrew prayers than I do. When I go back to Atlanta to see my parents and siblings, I am amazed at how the Temple has embraced Jewish ritual and Hebrew. Rabbi Marx, the one who banned *chuppah* weddings after the lynching of Leo Frank, would be appalled at the overt invitation to anti-Semitism in all that Jewishness.

And yet I would venture to say that all the accoutrements of Judaism have not lifted the spirituality of my coreligionists a bit. We are in a golden age of going through the motions, but we have made no real progress in grounding the People of Israel in a moral purpose. Our return to religiosity is tactical, borne of a desire to connect a wandering Jewish people to the synagogue and to identity. But while it has given many Jews an aura of authenticity, it has not enriched our theology.

As Rabbi Zemel put it, "This is a moment that's ripe for a Jewish voice in the public square, but we don't know what to say."

And now we have an existential threat to propel us into the square.

"There's been this debate forever and the debate has always been, how much do we really need to care about anti-Semitism?" Rabbi Roston said. "A generation or two before me, everyone looked back at beating Hitler. They wanted to fight the Holocaust. I wanted to look forward.

"But now we have an obligation to work against this. I think it's about Jewish survival. We don't want Jews to feel like we need to hide. That's not just religious. It's American, right?"

Beyond Jewish institutions, Jews ourselves are holding us back. American Jewry is bifurcating into a broad mass of increasingly irreligious secularists and a smaller, ardently tribalist orthodoxy. The Pew Research Center's Religion and Public Life division chronicled just that. In 2013, there were about 5.3 million Jewish adults and 1.3 million children being raised at least partly Jewish. But of those adults, 22 percent called themselves "Jews of no religion," and this number has grown with each generation: 32 percent of millennial Jews say they have no religion. Of the Jews with no religion who have children at home, two-thirds say their kids are being raised to have no Jewish identity in any way. In contrast, Orthodox

Jews—who tend to be politically conservative, tribalist, and fecund—are holding firm and strong. Those trends portend "a sharply declining non-Orthodox population in the second half of the twenty-first century, and a rising fraction of Jews who are Orthodox," Steven M. Cohen, a sociologist of American Jewry at Hebrew Union College–Jewish Institute of Religion, told the *New York Times*.

The Jews who are most interested in a liberal, internationalist future, who wish to live progressive, assimilated existences free of threat, are disappearing. Those willing to accept the rising tribalism—to keep to themselves and fortify the Jewish state as an escape hatch or fallout shelter—are growing in number.

It has been this way for five thousand years, Jonah Pesner says, sighing, reminding me that despite his jeans and fashionably narrow-cut shirt, he is a rabbi. Jews have had our liberal internationalists and our wall-building tribalists. Ezra returned to Jerusalem from Babylonian exile to discover, in horror, that Jewish men had been marrying non-Jewish women. He rent his garments, dissolved the *shiksa* marriages, and demanded that the Jews of Jerusalem obey the laws of the Torah. His prophet-in-arms, Nehemiah, the cupbearer of the Persian king Artaxerxes, went to Judea as governor, tasked with rebuilding what remained of the Jewish lands. His first move was to resurrect the walls around Jerusalem, purify the Jewish community, and rid the land of Samaritans, Ammonites, Arabs, and Philistines.

STAND UP OR IGNORE

If Ezra and Nehemiah were the ancient precursors of today's Jewish tribalists, Isaiah and Micah saw the beauty and breadth in humanity. "Holy, holy, holy is the Lord of Hosts; the whole earth is full of his glory!" the seraphim told Isaiah. Micah castigated the people of Israel for their corruption, their cruelty to the poor, and their oppression of the weak.

Hear this, I pray you, ye heads of the House of Jacob, and princes of the House of Israel, who abhor justice and make crooked all that is straight; who built up Zion with blood-guilt, and Jerusalem with wrong. Her leaders judge for bribe, and her priests teach for hire, and her prophets divine for money. And yet they will lean upon God and say: "Is not the Lord among us? Evil cannot befall us." Therefore, for your sake shall Zion be ploughed up like a field, and Jerusalem shall become ruinous heaps, and the mount of the Temple—forest-covered heights.

And when the people cried out for forgiveness and asked what they should do—present burnt offerings, sacrifice "thousands of rams, with myriads of streams of oil," offer their first-born children—the prophet replied, "He has told thee, man, what is good and what the Lord requires of thee. Only to do justly, and to love kindness, and to walk humbly with thy God."

Though Jerusalem may be destroyed, ultimately the swords will be beaten into plowshares and peace will reign on earth.

"Then shall every man sit under his vine and under his fig tree, with none to make them afraid; for the mouth of the Lord of Hosts has spoken. Though all the people walk each one in the name of his god, we shall walk in the name of God, our Lord, for ever and ever."

After all the fighting is done, after the arguments between the tribalists and the internationalists subside with weariness or laryngitis, one contextual narrative remains for the Jewish people, as Rabbi Pesner reminds us: "You shall love a stranger, for you were a stranger in the Land of Egypt."

How to love is all that needs to be resolved.

FIVE

Toward a Collective Response

A legend in progressive Jewish circles goes something like this. Kivie Kaplan, a young Jewish man in a hurry, was in South Florida with a black driver when he pulled up to a country club with a sign that read "No Jews or Dogs Allowed." Appalled, he turned to his driver, who shrugged and said, "Mr. Kaplan, they don't even bother listing Negroes." So incensed was Kaplan that he devoted himself, his business acumen, and his money to civil rights, joining the NAACP and rising to become its president. He purchased a stately mansion in Washington on Embassy Row and turned it over to the newly formed Religious Action Center of Reform Judaism. It was in that building's wood-paneled conference room, around its heavy, dark table, that African American and Jewish lawyers and leaders sat down to write the first drafts of the civil rights and voting rights acts of the 1960s. It remains a hub of Jewish activism to this day.

As Jonah Pesner tells me the story of Kivie and his driver, he lets out a sob, overcome by the emotion of it.

"We can't get into this binary thing where it's either us or it's them," he said. Rising anti-Semitism cannot be fought in isolation from so many other forms of bigotry—against gay and transgender people, Latinos, Muslims, African Americans, or Asians.

That lesson—cooperation and collective action, not one-upmanship on the victimization scale—is apt, but the legend is not quite accurate. Kaplan himself told the story in *American Jewish History: A Primary Source Reader*, with a slightly different emphasis. On his way to a business trip in Central America in 1932, he had deposited his wife and mother in Miami Beach to see the sights. Upon his return, they wanted to show him the highlights of their South Florida sojourn.

Not being a sight-seer I suffered for the cause and went around, and during the course of the afternoon we saw a sign on a hotel that said "no dogs or Jews allowed." The Negro gentleman stopped the car. He thought that I was visibly perturbed by my facial expression, but I didn't react that way. I was glad to see the sign on that hotel because I knew that there were ninety-nine other hotels in the Miami Beach area that did accept Jews and dogs and that's the place where I would want to spend my money. But he thought I was hurt so he took out his wallet and he said, "Mr. Kaplan, you know we Negroes cannot go out after eight p.m. in Miami Beach without a permit." He took this permit out and showed me where he had a permit to go after eight p.m. Evidently he wasn't satisfied that this consoled me and I still had this serious face on, and he said, "You know, Mr. Kaplan, we Negroes cannot go swimming in the ocean." Well, being twenty-eight years of age, knowing that we Jews have suffered for 5,000 years, having had experiences with anti-Semitism all of my life since I was a kid, I compared the problems of the Jew in the United States with the problems of the Negro and I said, "Gee, they really have a problem." I went home and I thought about this and I immediately joined up with the NAACP.

In Kaplan's telling, he clearly recognized that for all the slights he had suffered, his plight paled in comparison with his driver's—that as a Jew, he had something to give, and what he would give would largely go to the cause of African American equality. He shed no tears for himself. He wasn't even particularly bothered. He just went to work.

I tell this version of the story not to stomp on Rabbi Pesner's more emotional recitation (the rabbi appropriately concluded that Kivie Kaplan's sympathies lay more with the driver than with the Jew), but to make a point: Jews have thousands of years of history to place any given moment in perspective. We have the resources to help, educate, and organize, but even now, next to the attacks on Muslim Americans, the roundups of Latino undocumented immigrants, the reversals of gay and transgender rights, and the violence perpetrated against black communities, anti-Semitism is not the worst affliction to beset the United States in the Trump era, nor was it in many past eras. Leo Frank's lynching was horrifying, but it was a singularity in the decades that saw so much Strange Fruit hanging from the trees of Dixie. Emmett Till's lynching was not in itself an unusual event; it became a pivot point for the civil rights movement because of his mother's defiant open-casket display of her son's suffering and the barbarity of racism. The bombing of the Temple was a jolt, but at the time hundreds of bombs were exploding or fizzling in the homes of black pastors and civil rights leaders and in black churches and other black institutions. Fifty dynamite explosions between 1947 and 1965 earned the city of Birmingham, Alabama, the nickname "Bombingham." On June 10, 2017, in more than twenty cities across the country, an anti-Muslim group calling itself Act for America organized "Marches against Sharia" to protest the fantastical notion that the United States was being infiltrated by advocates of Islamic religious law. No one is organizing Marches against Mitzvahs.

But hate begets hate. Steep increases in hate crimes against foreign-born minorities throughout the 2016 campaign, and especially after the Trump triumph, are well documented. The

Center for the Study of Hate and Extremism, a nonpartisan research center at California State University, San Bernardino, found that across eight major metropolitan areas, hate crimes rose more than 20 percent in 2016, a significantly more dramatic yearly increase than any other since it began compiling statistics in 2010. Much of that violence was aimed at Muslims, Latinos, and immigrants, but in New York City hate crimes against blacks and Jews spiked between March 2016 and March 2017. In Los Angeles, was the n-word was spray-painted on the gate outside NBA star LeBron James's mansion. That same week, in Richmond, Virginia, a swastika was slapped on a Jewish Community Center. The Anti-Defamation League's tally of a 34 percent increase in anti-Semitic assaults, vandalism, and harassment in 2016 over 2015 is more than matched by the numbers of the Council on American-Islamic Relations. CAIR counted a 57 percent increase in anti-Muslim bias incidents in 2016 over 2015 and a 44 percent increase in anti-Muslim hate crimes. And where Jews report taunts and disruptions, bomb threats and spray paint, Muslim Americans are dealing with murder. A mosque was burned in Florida. "Muhammad: Prophet of Butchers" was spray-painted on the wall of the Muslim Community Center of Kingston, Rhode Island. Anti-Muslim protesters in Austin, Texas, carried signs reading "God Bless America & Israel." Following Election Day, around thirty mosques received the same letter: "To the children of Satan: You Muslims are a vile and filthy people. Your mothers and your fathers are dogs. You are evil.

You worship the devil. But your day of reckoning has arrived. There's a new sheriff in town—President Donald Trump. He's going to cleanse America and make it shine again. And he's going to start with you Muslims. He's going to do to you Muslims what Hitler did to the Jews."

But also this: seventeen-year-old Nabra Hassanen was beaten to death with a metal baseball bat in June 2017, her body thrown into a pond in an affluent suburb of Washington, after leaving a mosque after late prayers during Ramadan. Deah Shaddy Barakat, Yusor Mohammad Abu-Salha, and Razan Mohammad Abu-Salha were gunned down in their home in Chapel Hill, North Carolina, in 2015 by an "Atheist for Equality." And the list goes on. Neo-Nazis threatened to march through Whitefish and menace the town's Jews but didn't. In late July 2017, in a remote hamlet in the Catskills called Islamberg, founded by African American Muslims, they actually showed up. Right-wingers clad in militia uniforms descended on the village to intimidate the inhabitants.

"This is a war," declared Gavin McInnes, founder of the alt-right "Proud Boys" and contributor to the pro-Trump website InfoWars.

For all the dog whistles that anti-Semites say they heard from Team Trump, the Islamophobes heard bullhorns. "Islam hates us," Trump said in an interview on *Anderson Cooper 360* in March 2016. He would "certainly" implement a database of Muslim Americans, a people for whom there has been "no real assimilation." After an Islamic State sympathizer gunned down forty-nine revelers at an Orlando nightclub, candidate Trump falsely asserted, "They have to cooperate with law enforcement and turn in the people who they know are bad. . . . But you know what? They didn't turn them in. And you know what? We had death and destruction."

Not to mention that African American motorists continue to be gunned down by police with utter impunity. The shooting of Philando Castile, streamed live on Facebook by his distraught girlfriend, shocked the conscience of the nation. Only after the policeman who shot Castile was acquitted did we see the dashboard camera footage of him firing seven bullets into Castile with no provocation. Remarkably, we were less shocked the second go-round. By the summer of 2017, a new old evil had emerged with the appearance of nooses around the country: at the Philadelphia Mint; on a tree outside the Hirshhorn Museum and in a gallery at the recently opened National Museum of African American History and Culture in Washington; at a middle school in Florida and a high school in North Carolina; at a frat house at the University of Maryland and on the campus of American University in Washington; and in the whiter reaches of the District of Columbia. For black America, those loops of rope were horrifying threats and a reminder that not everyone in the United States misses the bad old days of lynch law.

And for all the hand-wringing about the wording of Trump's International Holocaust Remembrance Day statement, the entire month of June 2017 came and went without even an acknowledgment by the White House of LGBT Pride Month. Not a peep.

As Kivie Kaplan would say, "Gee, they really have a problem." Then he'd get to work.

We're all in this together.

But what does collective action look like? And how should displays of solidarity be handled in ways that do not give megaphones to the bigots and the haters? When Richard Spencer led his first march of white nationalists in Charlottesville to protest the removal of a Confederate memorial—the one before the march that turned bloody—the khaki-clad gathering looked vaguely ludicrous carrying tiki torches and chanting "Russia is our friend." At times like that, it is easy to dismiss the alt-right as pathetic. A video set to the tune of Billy Joel's "We Didn't Start the Fire," featuring a stream of names in the movement, film clips of right-wing European marches, and a middle-aged white nationalist, Jared Taylor, playing the saxophone briefly, became a laughingstock on YouTube—hardly Leni Riefenstahl. Even after the deadly Charlottesville melee in August 2017, mainstream conservatives were quick to label the anti-Semitic white supremacists as losers, hoping that a dismissive insult would negate the power they might hold over impressionable and angry bystanders.

The coverage of all of this has made me queasy. Spencer

has seized the megaphone, and the media is there to amplify his message. The anarchists of Antifa have expanded the reach of the alt-right's message and perhaps exaggerated its strength by turning even the smallest gathering into violent street theater. The organizers of the Charlottesville "Unite the Right" march left the bloody streets of the historic town vowing to expand the movement while the spotlight was on them.

Still, something must be done. This is not an exhortation to promise the pursuit of social justice. At any given synagogue on any given Friday night, a rabbi will deliver a sermon on gun control or community solidarity or fighting poverty. And to what end? Rabbi Pesner talks of going to the Reform Judaism youth group NFTY as a teenager in New York in the 1980s and hearing incessant calls for social justice. Then he would take public transportation to the Bronx High School of Science, past grinding poverty, hopelessness, and anger, and wonder at the meaning of social justice and marches on Washington when such unrelenting misery was all around him.

"This can't just be about what's happening in Washington," he says. "It has to be about the Bronx, and Roxbury, and Dorchester. We're all in a fight to reclaim the country."

But are we? Do we know that yet, or are we still grappling more with signs of social deterioration and wondering where they might lead, like those Jews who feared waves of pogroms after the Republican Revolution of 1994? Are we in a momentary blip of resurgent intolerance, a last gasp of ethno-nationalism that will recede to the inevitable advance of liberal

internationalism? Or will historians look back at the post–
World War II era as the exception to a human history of warring tribes?

As a teenager, I briefly joined the staunchly Zionist youth
group Young Judea, not really out of any fervent desire to make
aliyah—moving to Israel to join the faithful in my homeland—
but more out of a desire to date Nancy Berlin (never realized).
Our chapter was called *Ko'ach*—"strength" in Hebrew—and
we talked a lot about Israel. But when one of the girls in *Ko'ach*
said she couldn't wait to graduate from high school and move
to the Jewish state to leave a nation that could never accept
her, I laughed. I still do. America does not hate Jews, though
some Americans do.

David Saperstein is willing to concede that he does not
know the answers to these questions. In the 1920s and 1930s,
long before there was anything that could be labeled a civil
rights movement, African American academics began carefully researching the impact of segregation and Jim Crow
on children, poverty, and society writ large. Lawyers, many of
them Jewish, debated whether to tackle discrimination on a
case-by-case basis or build a grand case that would render Jim
Crow a legal abomination. In those early days of civil rights,
the approach was meticulous and methodical. Franklin Roosevelt's progressive attorney general, Frank Murphy, recruited
two Jewish lawyers, Albert Arent and Irwin Langbein, to
help form a new Civil Liberties Unit in the Justice Department's criminal division in 1939, the precursor to the Division

of Civil Rights. Most civil rights statutes enacted during Reconstruction had long been repealed or declared unconstitutional by unfriendly Supreme Courts. The federal government had not shown any interest in prosecuting the predations of the Ku Klux Klan or racist police forces, nor did its attorneys have the legal tools to do so if they had wished.

With Murphy's blessing, Arent and Langbein paged through musty federal statutes looking for ways to wrest civil rights enforcement from the states. They found two Reconstruction-era statutes, then drafted a thirty-one-page memo for all U.S. Attorneys in the department. Dry, yes, but significant, because Arent and Langbein had put the Department of Justice on record as favoring the application of federal law to prosecute lynching, mob violence, and other violations of civil liberties and had found, or created, the legal weapons to pursue justice. They and black lawyers like Thurgood Marshall began taking cases to court, learning from wins and losses, until *Brown v. Board of Education* could provide the One Big Case in 1954.

That, to Saperstein, is where we stand: watch the rise of hate, monitor, and test legal theories. A declaration of war against a changed social order? "We're not there, or at least I'm not there," he told me.

But like responding to climate change, building alliances against hate can hardly hurt, even if it turns out our worst fears were a tad alarmist. A rabbi in Israel, intent on making me a religious Jew, told me when I was twenty that an agnostic who did not follow Jewish law religiously is a fool. Yes, maybe there is no God, but if there was the slightest chance that God did exist and that He demanded fealty to the laws He gave to Moses, why take the risk of refusing? Well, the price of his logic was too high for me. I like cheeseburgers and pepperoni pizza and Friday nights out too much to comply.

But that's not what we're talking about here. The logic of climate denial—of doing nothing as we watch and wait for those rising seas, searing droughts, and worsening storms—collapses when you look at the remedies for climate agnosticism. If we move to an efficient, clean-energy economy that relies on solar, wind, and other renewables to replace the burning of fossil fuels, sure, it could raise our energy costs a bit; it will undoubtedly hurt coal miners and eventually frackers and wildcatters in the pastures of North Dakota and the hills of western Pennsylvania. But a cleaner, more technologically sophisticated energy sector would be worth it, regardless of whether climate change is real or not, regardless of whether you believe global warming is an existential threat or an inconvenience.

Ditto the kind of efforts required to confront the alt-right. Allying internationalist Jews with concerned moderate Muslims, tolerant Christians, and anyone else willing to stand in solidarity against hate and intolerance is a good thing, regardless of the threat that Richard Spencer or Andrew Anglin poses. Bolstering public education falls into the same category. Better-educated citizens are less likely to hate. They are also more likely to succeed. Just do it.

"If we lose the public schools in America, we've lost America," Rabbi Saperstein told me.

And now is the time. If the alt-right moves from provocation, Internet shenanigans, and the occasional unplanned melee to organized violence and physical intimidation, strategies of cooperation and solidarity fall away fast as law enforcement takes over. Then it is no more in our hands than battling drug cartels or criminal gangs. The nation divides into warring camps with little prospect of communication. A recent ad by the National Rifle Association hinted at what might be coming, with an angry female narrator, the conservative commentator Dana Loesch, castigating the violent Left, angrily staring into the camera, and pledging resistance with "the clenched fist of truth" as images of anarchist rage skitter over the screen. Clenched fists are difficult to reach out to.

The response to the alt-right must, in some sense, be modeled after the alt-right itself: a blend of very old attitudes in very new technological clothing. Yes, there are lessons from the civil rights era: the formation of interracial, interfaith alliances; the development of legal theory and the taking of legal action; street demonstrations and resistance. This is, in fact, already happening—in San José, California; Gastonia, North Carolina; and Nashville, Tennessee, among other places. A handful of clergy founded Nashville Organized for Action and Hope, or NOAH, in 2013. It is now up to sixty-two organizations, mainly Protestant churches, black and white, but also two synagogues, two Muslim groups, two Unitarian congregations, seven labor unions, two Catholic churches, and one Catholic organization, said the Reverend Ed Thompson, its leader. With so many issues confronting Nashville—police brutality, school disciplinary problems, a lack of affordable housing, environmental degradation that came with the city's topsy-turvy growth—the group decided to hold an "issues convention" in 2014 to narrow its mission. NOAH emerged with three main issues and an interracial, interfaith coalition to deal with them: affordable housing and gentrification, criminal justice, and economic equity and jobs. And it's showing results. NOAH secured $25 million in Nashville's budget to buy some newly renovated properties to secure for low-income residents. It pressed for and got body cameras and dashboard cameras for the Nashville police force. And its leaders are spreading their model to Chattanooga, Memphis, Knoxville, and Oak Ridge.

"It helps tremendously having a diverse, multiracial, interfaith group. It gives us clout when people can see we're not all black, we're not all white," Reverend Thompson told me. "When we first started, the Chamber of Commerce put a death sentence on us. They said we wouldn't last but six months. Now they've started asking us to come talk to them."

Although the alt-right per se is not one of its chosen targets, NOAH is taking notice of rising hate. In June 2017 the community hosted a public forum titled "Guiding Faith Communities in Challenging Times." Pat Halper, a leader of the group who converted to Judaism nearly three decades ago, was attacked for her role in such a "leftist" organization by Christians who maintain they are better for the Jews than she is. Why? Because she had the audacity to align with Muslims. "Political leftists seem to dominate the organized Jewish community in Nashville, Tennessee," harrumphed the Islamophobic website Gates of Vienna in April 2016. "Despite over 100 knife attacks on Jews in Israel, no matter how many calls for intifada, no matter how many Jewish children are murdered while sleeping in their beds, politically left American Jews and their leadership stand with the jihadist murderers." Again, Israel is the obsession, the wedge, the diversion from problems and solutions at home.

Halper shrugs off the attacks. "For me, and some other Jewish people that I know, Israel is Israel. They are running that country. There is so much to do in this country," she told me. "My thoughts and efforts are focused here."

But she is no Pollyanna about NOAH's efforts in Nashville, which so many times are exhortations to the amen chorus. "A lot of times, I do feel like we're preaching to the choir," she said. Both Halper and Thompson conceded that NOAH is having a very hard time reaching out to the city's growing immigrant population, especially Latinos, who are flocking to Nashville but remain marginalized and segregated. "But the reason I do what I do is exemplifying the way we should live," she said. "It's acknowledging each other's humanity, it's civil discourse, welcoming the stranger. We have to live our values."

So how are those gaps bridged? How are the new victims reached and the new perpetrators addressed? The new battle-field is not just in ghettoized urban enclaves and rural redoubts of prejudice. It's very much online. For an older generation, that might seem meaningless—turn off the computer, delete your Twitter account, pick up a book. Younger readers, how-ever, will sympathize with Zoë Quinn, who told me, "Okay, so I'm not supposed to do my job? I am a programmer and an artist. If you're not on social media, you're dead in the water. That's like saying don't leave your house because there are people lighting your lawn on fire. Focus on the people burn-ing your fucking lawn."

The world online—for video-game developers like Zoë Quinn, for journalists, for pretty much everyone today—is as much a part of the world as the Starbucks down the street.

Let's revisit Gamergate, the first manifestation of alt-right cyber-harassment-cum-stalking, and Zoë Quinn's response. Quinn didn't lie low. She and her then boyfriend but current business partner, Alex Lifschitz, founded Crash Override, a support service for victims, social workers, lawyers, and secu-rity experts dealing with Internet abuse. Crash Override—also the name of Quinn's book—offers practical tools to strike back against cyber thugs: software tools to protect victims; advice on how to protect personal records that could be used for doxing or swatting (the lovely, potentially deadly practice of phoning in false 911 calls claiming that dire activities are occurring at a given address—active shooter, weapons spotted, and so on—often triggering the dispatching of a SWAT team to the target's house), legal referrals, and partnerships with tech companies like Twitter, which could be more active in combating social-network thuggery. A caller who gets in touch with Quinn is first asked how far the abuse has gone. If it's just harassment but not yet doxing, she walks the victim through exactly how to get personal information scrubbed from social media sites, how to change passwords, and how to delete dormant accounts.

"Small actionable tasks have a good effect on people in crisis, changing passwords, removing personal information that we've found," she explained. "I actually made an interactive tool to step-by-step go through social media accounts. Do you have an Amazon account? Click this link, check your setting, if it's this, you probably want to change it. Being centered, having a task, and having that task not be overwhelming—that's key."

If the attack has already progressed to the finding and publication of personal information, the next question is, "Is the information that's out there accurate? Is there any more to be had? If so, let's scrub it immediately." If the information is accurate, Crash Override has what it calls "escalation channels," people in law enforcement with whom Quinn and Lifschitz have built relationships and who understand the malevolence of online assailants. Quinn and Lifschitz have figured out that you never call a police station and mention emails, the Internet, user names, doxing, or swatting. The police won't take it seriously. Keep it simple. "A prank call could be coming in reporting a terrible crime at this address. Please, keep your guns down. We know you have to take reports of ongoing assault seriously, but this will be a prank." By giving local police stations that heads-up, Zoë says they've prevented several swattings (and probably saved the lives of a few dogs, which tend to greet cops with guns drawn in an unfriendly way and end up shot— ah, the things you learn from dealing with the alt-right). In all this, the victim guides the response.

"The thing with online and offline abuse is, it's fundamentally about controlling someone else. The last thing you want to do is take agency away from the people who are being attacked: 'Here are the avenues open to us. Here are some likely outcomes. Whatever you want to do is up to you. We don't want to pressure you.' The last thing to do is force someone into the shitty position of having to be the one who fights back," she told me.

In 2015, the first year of Crash Override's hotline, Zoë Quinn told me she personally handled a thousand calls. And that was before the Trump-era alt-right. She eventually had to shut down the phone hotline ("Dealing with Nazis all the time has an effect on you"), though there is an email "crisis line." She's now trying to figure out how to monetize the effort, hire professionals, and actually incorporate—not to make money, but because private companies are afforded secrecy protections that nonprofits aren't. Privacy is of the essence if you are battling a foe that uses publicity as its primary weapon.

Zoë Quinn's response is not exactly a how-to for the anti-alt-right. A lot of the people who have reached out to Crash

Override are not like the Jews of Whitefish, a certain class of victim targeted by an organized electronic pogrom. They are transgender kids bullied by their schoolmates, gay teens struggling with abuse and their own self-doubt, or—a particular breed in the Internet era—women targeted by ex-boyfriends with "revenge porn" (the posting of sexual images without consent). They are also just anyone—targets of cyberstalkers, harassers, or hackers who are empowered by the tools of the Internet in an era when privacy is more wishful thinking than reality. "We have completely boring straight white men, nothing that would make a hate group interested in them," she marvels. "You said something embarrassing, they don't like the way you look, you were nice to a marginalized person—and they'll come after you." The hate she deals with is more ancient than anti-Semitism, more ancient than Judaism. It's as ancient as Cain and Abel. It's personal.

During Gamergate, a friend of hers decided he would defend her by aggressively confronting her tormentors and promoting the games she designs and sells. For his efforts, his website was hacked and his personal identification, including his Social Security number, was stolen, as was his wife's. Don't be fooled. The enemy is powerful. And he doesn't really like to be trifled with.

Yair Rosenberg, a senior writer for the online Jewish magazine Tablet, loves to joust with his alt-right tormentors. "Anti-Semitism doesn't exist because Judaism is a social construct," one alt-righter told him on Twitter. He responded,

"But if the koala can dance with the mamba, who will consort with the cashew?" To which "St. Frexit" responded, "Why do Jewish men like to watch porno movies backwards? They like the part where the hooker gives the money back." Rosenberg replied, "Of piranhas and pierogies, who can know? A paradox of porpoises." Yair seems to be enjoying himself, but to what end?

Zoë Quinn, on the other hand, has much to teach us. If Gamergate had happened in, say, 2007 instead of 2014, she told me, she would have been on the wrong side, joining the tormentors. She actually participated in 4chan-driven hacks on the Church of Scientology as a lark. She fully participated in the crass, misogynist culture of the gaming world before she became its victim. To show she wasn't some softhearted social justice warrior or special snowflake, she greeted guy gamers with the same taunt that they greeted women gamers, "Tits or GTFO"—short for "Show us your tits or get the fuck out." She knows the enemy and knows what works. Talking to them doesn't, Quinn maintains. They may sound receptive, might engage you, but they will then use the interaction as a trophy: "I got her to talk. I'm so cool." Instead, she works through more professional channels, educating law enforcement about the threat, stressing that it is real, talking to members of Congress, state legislators, executives in social media companies and software firms like Twitter, Facebook, and Google. She even brought the issue to the United Nations. It starts, she says, with getting them to take the troll armies seriously.

A video-game publisher who had previously laughed off Gamer-gate eventually called the actions of its perpetrators a hate crime. That was worth celebrating—quietly.

"I know progress is going to move at a fucking iceberg pace, but it is nice to see," Zoë allowed.

If Zoë Quinn, a rainbow-haired video-game designer with a tiny firm in California, can accomplish all that she has, imagine what the Anti-Defamation League could do—or, better yet, the American Jewish Committee, or the Jewish Federations of North America, or the Conference of Presidents of Major American Jewish Organizations, or, hell, AIPAC. Jewish organizational strength and Jewish resources, legal know-how, and media savvy could build out from Crash Over-ride, erect a powerful infrastructure for online awareness and response, harness existing channels between groups like the Anti-Defamation League and the FBI, and use legal channels to dismantle or bankrupt hate groups that attack. We could build the body of law needed for the Internet age, either through legal precedent or legislative effort. And, most im-portant, we could regain our voice in the public square, making injustice our primary focus.

The early efforts by the Anti-Defamation League into the alt-right arena are already showing promise, if the squealing is any indication. In the summer of 2016 the ADL posted an online guide to the alt-right/alt-lite—a relatively innocuous list of the main figures in the movement with thumbnail biog-raphies and sketches of actions they had taken. The unhinged response was as revelatory as it was hilarious. Mike Cernovich was one of the leaders of the Gamergate swarm who made his name as an online misogynist bully and then remade himself into a "journalist" for the Trump era. He ranted, "The ADL has targeted me for murder and assassination. Today they released a hate list identifying me as some kind of purveyor of hate or something like that." His wild eyes were incongruous with the backdrop of a pleasant-looking park as he streamed. "They're trying to get me murdered. The ADL is trying to get me murdered. There's no question what they're doing." Never mind that the guide "From Alt Right to Alt Lite: Naming the Hate" in no way named precisely where the players on the Right lived and worked. It did not identify their families or publish phone numbers, email addresses, Social Security numbers, or addresses, or otherwise order an army of Jews and anti-fascists to attack them. Never mind Cernovich's own history: He joined the Gamergate fray as the lawyer defending Zoë Quinn's ex-boyfriend in his desire to destroy her. He is also no stranger to the art of doxing his detractors. The Anti-Defamation League had not done to the alt-right what the alt-right was perfectly willing to do to anyone else. But the response, ironic as it was, showed panic—and perhaps a glass jaw—in the face of an organized response.

Carrying that response further would take a recalibration, a conscious move away from the Israel obsession of the largest Jewish institutions and a recognition that tribalism is leading Jewry into a box canyon crowded with some unsavory characters from the ethno-nationalist movement. That old Left bumper sticker pretty much had it right: think globally, act locally. The Trump campaign was also right: We are the globalists. Embrace it.

Recall Richard Spencer's invocation of Fukuyama's "End of History" and his exhortation to his followers to use white nationalism to restart history—to impose meaning and struggle after those defining organizational principles were lost to the end of the Cold War. He had a point. Fukuyama himself concluded that, "The end of history will be a sad time.

"The struggle for recognition, the willingness to risk one's life for a purely abstract goal, the worldwide ideological struggle that called forth daring, courage, imagination, and idealism, will be replaced by economic calculations, the endless solving of technical problems, environmental concerns, and the satisfaction of sophisticated consumer demands. . . . Perhaps this very prospect of centuries of boredom at the end of history will serve to get history started once again."

Better that we restart it than Spencer and his ilk. We have been warned.

Indeed, ever since Robert Kagan wrote that column in the *Washington Post* in May 2016 on the coming authoritarianism, writers and activists have been warning us of the arrival of fascism to American shores. David Frum, a former George W. Bush speechwriter, penned a convincing piece for the *Atlantic* titled "How to Build an Autocracy" that took readers step-by-step through the lulling of the electorate, with bread (tax cuts, big spending, roaring deficits, and a soaring stock market) and circuses (a compliant media, endless entertainment) to accept a crony kleptocracy where freedom is willingly sacrificed for nationalist ego-stroking and an endless rise in our 401(k) plans:

Donald Trump will not set out to build an authoritarian state. His immediate priority seems likely to be to use the presidency to enrich himself. But as he does so, he will need to protect himself from legal risk. Being Trump, he will also inevitably wish to inflict payback on his critics. Construction of an apparatus of impunity and revenge will begin haphazardly and opportunistically. But it will accelerate. It will have to.

Timothy Snyder, in his brief jeremiad *On Tyranny*, published in February 2017, raises the concept of "anticipatory obedience," describing the famous experiment by Yale University psychologist Stanley Milgram in the early 1960s, when he recruited Yale students and random New Haven residents and told them to apply electric shocks to people whom they did not know who were part of the experiment on the other side of a window.

As the subjects (thought they) shocked the (people they thought were) participants in a learning experiment, they saw a horrible sight. People whom they did not know, and against whom they had no grievance, seemed to be suffering greatly—pounding the glass and complaining of heart pain. Even so, most subjects followed Milgram's instructions and continued to apply (what they thought were) ever greater shocks until the victims appeared to die. Even those who did not proceed all the way to the (apparent) killing of their fellow human beings left without inquiring about the health of the other participants.

We are, it would seem, cattle waiting compliantly to be herded to an autocratic future.

But in the brief time that Donald J. Trump has been president, the American people feel anything but docile. Barricades surround the Trump International Hotel in Washington to contain the constant protests. Demonstrations spontaneously erupt at airports. "Resist" is a far more potent slogan than Cernovich's #ADLTerror or the National Rifle Association's Clenched Fist of Truth. The Internet, late-night television, bars, and comedy clubs crackle with mockery, irreverence, anger, and alarm. It just doesn't feel like Americans are lining up in "anticipatory obedience" to offer our services to the state to round up illegal immigrants, prevent Muslims from entering the country, smash the pot dispensaries of Obama's debauched America, burn books, and boycott the Jews.

But while so many Americans seem sure of what they are against, they are not as confident about what they are for.

American Jews need to assert a voice in the public arena, to back our institutions and mold them in our image. Jewish leadership must reflect its congregants, who are not sheep. When the Anti-Defamation League released its guide to the alt-right/alt-lite, Ohio state treasurer Josh Mandel, who is Republican and Jewish, and is again running for the Senate, actually backed Mike Cernovich and another figure in that world who was not on the ADL list, Jack Posobiec. "Sad to see @ADL_National become a partisan witchhunt group targeting people for political beliefs. I stand with @Cernovich & @JackPosobiec," Mandel proclaimed on Twitter above a link to Cernovich's screed charging that the ADL was trying to have him killed.

I will grant that neither Cernovich nor Posobiec is in the Richard Spencer–Andrew Anglin category of publishers of outright racist or anti-Semitic rhetoric. But Cernovich advocates I.Q. tests for immigrants, "no white guilt," and is an unapologetic misogynist. "Have you guys ever tried 'raping' a girl without using force?" he asked on Twitter in 2012. "Try it. It's basically impossible. Date rape does not exist." And speaking of racism, he offered this bit of altruism: "Not being a slut is the only proven way to avoid AIDS. If you love black women, slut shame them." In the summer of 2017, Cernovich may well have crossed over into neo-Nazi territory when he circulated a cartoon depicting White House national security adviser H. R. McMaster and retired general David Petraeus as dancing marionettes, with George Soros pulling their strings, while a disembodied, wrinkled hand labeled "Rothschilds" pulls the strings attached to Soros. The alt-right's campaign against McMaster had skidded into outright anti-Semitism.

Posobiec has been one of the promulgators of truly fake news: that Hillary Clinton helped run a child sex ring in the back of a pizza parlor; that a young Democratic National Committee staff member, Seth Rich, was murdered by the Clinton campaign; and that former attorney general Loretta Lynch had called for "blood in the streets" shortly before a would-be assassin opened fire on a Congressional practice baseball game in suburban Washington. He also planted "Rape Melania" signs at anti-Trump rallies to sully the Resistance and disrupted a Shakespeare in the Park production of *Julius Caesar* that he claimed was a call to assassinate Trump. Amid the furor over Trump's tepid, confused response to Charlottesville, the President of the United States gave a coveted retweet to Posobiec when the trickster tried to deflect attention to another bloody weekend in Chicago—still more evidence that Trump is wading in some filthy online waters.

For drawing attention to these men, the Anti-Defamation League was somehow tarred as a liberal, partisan organization by an elected Jewish Republican—the essence of an assault on a century-old Jewish institution. I did not see any organized effort to rally around the institution. Why is that significant?

The question brings to mind a haunting passage from a Jewish newspaper in Berlin, written in 1933 and quoted by Timothy Snyder in *On Tyranny*.

> We do not subscribe to the view that Mr. Hitler and his friends, now finally in possession of the power they have so long desired, will implement the proposals circulating in [Nazi newspapers]; they will not suddenly deprive German Jews of their constitutional rights, nor enclose them in ghettos, nor subject them to the jealous and murderous impulses of the mob. They cannot do this because a number of crucial factors hold powers in check . . . and they clearly do not want to go down that road. When one acts as a European power, the whole atmosphere tends towards ethical reflection upon one's better self and away from revisiting one's earlier oppositional posture.

Institutions matter, but they do not survive on their own. They must be defended, and at the moment, the Anti-Defamation League is an institution under concerted, partisan attack and is not being defended.

Truth also needs to be defended, and groups like the Anti-Defamation League and the Southern Poverty Law Center try to defend truth as they expose hate. To most of us, at least for now, the notion that Hillary Clinton and her campaign manager, John Podesta, ran a pedophile ring in the back of

Comet Ping Pong, on a busy commercial strip in Washington's affluent Northwest quadrant, is absurd. So is the tall tale that Seth Rich, a young Democratic National Committee staffer who was tragically murdered in a gentrifying part of Washington before dawn in 2016, was rubbed out by Democrats because he was leaking emails to the Russians. But in the alternative universe of the alt-right, these stories are taken as truth—not because the haters in the alt-right have found logic in these stories but because they feed the larger narrative of a debauched world of liberalism that needs cleansing by fire. Even after a disturbed man from North Carolina showed up with a gun at Comet Ping Pong to free the enslaved children and nearly caused a real tragedy, the promulgators of Pizzagate like Mike Cernovich offered no mea culpas or apologies. The lies are too valuable to the larger movement.

I had the privilege in August 2017 of seeing a revival of Eugene Ionesco's play *Rhinoceros* at the Edinburgh International Festival. There was good reason why an absurdist play from 1959 was being given such prominence at one of Europe's preeminent arts festivals. Ionesco had watched helplessly in the 1930s as, one by one, the university professors, students, and intellectuals around him abandoned logic and took up first the language, then the beliefs of Nazism in his native Romania. Standing out was too difficult, too risky. Ionesco wrote: "From time to time, one of our friends said: 'I don't agree with them, to be sure, but on certain points, nevertheless, I must admit, for example, the Jews . . . ,' etc. And this was a symptom. Three weeks later, this person would become a Nazi. He was caught in the mechanism, he accepted everything, he became a rhinoceros." In the play, one by one, the people of a provincial French village are transformed into great horned pachyderms. "Give in to animal instincts," one of the main characters bellows as he smears gray clay over his face and hair. "Let's try to talk to them," says another. The absurd becomes the ubiquitous. No matter how ridiculous the logic, resistance is futile, until one character remains, still human, at first defiant, then morose and alone.

Why not stage *Rhinoceros* in Scotland, the land that created such insults to our president as "I hate Trump and everything he stands for. Whispy-haired [*sic*], leather faced, bawbag-eyed fuck bumper. ["Bawbag" is a Scots word for "scrotum" that is also slang for "coward."] He can take his golf course to fuck," and of course, the even more famous "Glaikit heidbanger. Brutal shan basturt. Manky great walloper. Total roaster. Heid-the-baw. Fud." The Edinburgh *Rhinoceros*, of course, was updated. The villagers debated the difference between rhinos from Europe and from the Middle East. A great gasp went up among the cast when one character accused another of being a migrant.

"Why aren't we discussing this phenomenon more?" the main character pleads. "We would be, say, if these events were happening in America." The audience laughed knowingly.

I do not mean to preach. In the great tide of public opinion, one person's opposition can feel pointless. The man who stood in front of the column of tanks on its way to Tiananmen Square created an iconic image, but in the end he had no choice but to make way. That said, we have seen that freedom really does feel bred in the American bone. When President Trump's "election integrity" project—led by Kris Kobach, who as Kansas secretary of state has been accused repeatedly of suppressing the vote—sought the voter rolls of every state, complete with partial Social Security numbers, the resistance was bipartisan. It was a deep-red Republican secretary of state in Mississippi who told Kobach to find a pier on his state's coast and jump in the Gulf of Mexico.

For Jews, this is personal. Had ordinary Germans and Poles and Ukrainians and Austrians and French people not played along, had consumers continued to shop in Jewish establishments and gotten their checkups with Jewish doctors, maybe, just maybe, history would have been altered even a little bit, and the Final Solution would not have been quite so final. To stand up to creeping totalitarianism, we needn't throw ourselves under the tank treads. We just need to not play the game. And refusal to play the game can be collective. If the vinyl banners proclaiming "Remember Darfur" that once graced the front of nearly every synagogue could give way to "We Stand with Israel," why can't they now give way to "We Stand against Hate"? Why can't the domestic apparatus of the American Jewish Committee reconstitute itself at the request of Jewish donors and members, and the Anti-Defamation League reassert itself, like the Southern Poverty Law Center, in the arena of bigotry without fear of being charged with partisanship?

And for God's sake, don't get exorcised about the fringe left at the Dyke March in Chicago when the orchestrators sit in the West Wing. Yes, anti-Israel sentiment is real on the Left, on campuses and in the Resistance, and some of it swerves beyond the bounds of political sentiment into anti-Semitism. But the real problem lies in the censorious reaction to the rising hatred of the alt-right, the sense that if we can't win the argument, we will shut it down.

In the early 1930s, before Hitler legitimately came to power, consolidated control, and burned the Reichstag, the Brownshirts clashed furiously with violent German Communists. At one point, it wasn't clear which side would prevail in these running street brawls. Germany could easily have swung far to the left to link arms with Stalin's Soviet Union. The German people largely stayed silent, shunning both factions, unable to take sides. That anarchic moment in history always comes to mind when I watch the black-clad, masked Antifa protesters preparing with relish for their showdowns with the khaki-wearing alt-right. Antifa cannot be allowed to represent the most vibrant form of resistance—not if the great mass of the American electorate is to join in. Nor can the student activists whose first method of confrontation is the heckler's veto. The cause of free speech must be returned to its pluralistic, open roots, not ceded to the promulgators of hate, seeking some purchase on a false moral high ground.

This is an era that calls for fearlessness, not heedlessness, but also for a refusal to play along. We as Jews are strong in our cohesion and have everything to gain in standing up for our commitment to liberal internationalism in the oldest, least partisan sense of that phrase—the sense that goes back to Disraeli and Mendelssohn and Maimonides. We are strong, but sadly, too many of us have taken advantage of that strength to retreat from collective conscience, to let justice be someone else's problem. And now, fear is creeping back in. My elder daughter asked me recently whether she looked Jewish. "Why?" I responded. "Because I don't want to. I don't want to be targeted like you are. I don't want to be afraid." It was probably of little use that I exhorted her to be proud of her heritage, to be Jewish in culture if not in religion, and to be unafraid. I should have responded with the words of Rabbi Arthur Hertzberg on the burden of the Chosen:

> There is no quiet life for Jews anywhere, at least not for long. The only question is whether one lives among the tempests with purpose and dignity. We Jews know why we suffer. Society resents anyone who challenges its fundamental beliefs, behavior, and prejudices. The ruling class does not like to be told that morality overrules power. The claim to chosenness guarantees that Jews live unquiet lives. I say it is far better to be the chosen people, the goad and the irritant to much of humanity, than to live timidly and fearfully. Jews exist to be bold.

Let's not get too self-congratulatory. Rabbi Hertzberg wrote of Jews as we should be, not as we are. Too many of us have assumed the trappings of the ruling class, accepted power and bent our morality to it—or forgotten morality altogether. Too many of us refuse to even speak of morality. A Jew who works in the Trump White House, when confronted with the works of Steve Bannon and Sebastian Gorka, shrugged it off with this: "There are assholes everywhere."

Jews have shown they do have a choice. The fact is, as my daughter grows, she will make that choice. Hiding is a statement. So is accommodation.

"Life is political," Timothy Snyder writes, "not because the world cares about how you feel, but because the world reacts to what you do."

The world is watching.

Acknowledgments

I am always in debt to my daughters, Hannah and Alissa, but when it comes to matters of religion, I am especially indebted— to my atheist who challenges me every day, and to my religious child, who has made Judaism a faith by choice.

For her patience and support, I thank Jennifer Steinhauer, the love of my life.

This book would not have happened without the encouragement of Rayhane Sanders, without the foresight of Karen Wolny, and without the diligence of the whole St. Martin's team.

I will be forever grateful to the rabbis who guided my thoughts and reading: David Saperstein, Jonah Pesner, Daniel Zemel, Sonny Schnitzer, and Francine Roston. I will be forever in awe of the brave women who have stood up to the bigots and thugs of the alt right, especially Zoë Quinn and Tanya Gersh.

ACKNOWLEDGMENTS

I would also like to thank someone I've never met, historian Timothy Snyder, whose graceful writing and keen insights may have done more to shape my conclusions than anyone else.

Notes

Introduction

3 *"You can leave them be"*: "Washington D.C. Free Speech Rally—Matthew Lyons (Full) (June 25th, 2017)," YouTube, July 5, 2017.

3 *"Instead of giving another paean to free speech"*: "Washington D.C. Free Speech Rally—Mike 'Enoch' Penovich (June 25th, 2017)," YouTube, July 5, 2017.

6–7 *"Get right with the leader . . . Meanwhile, don't alienate"*: Robert Kagan, "This Is How Fascism Comes to America," *Washington Post*, May 18, 2016.

16 *"I don't control my fans"*: Mickey Rapkin, "Lady and the Trump," *DuJour* (May 2016).

16 *"I have augmented my firearms collection"*: Bethany Mandel, "My Trump Tweets Earned Me So Many Anti-Semitic Haters I Bought a Gun," *Forward*, March 21, 2016.

17 *The Anti-Defamation League tasked a group of venerable reporters:* "ADL Report: Anti-Semitic Targeting of Journalists During the 2016 Presidential Campaign," a report from ADL's Task Force

on Harassment and Journalism, Anti-Defamation League, October 19, 2016.

20   *"making the lives of journalists":* Tina Nguyen, "Milo Yiannopoulos Is Starting a New, Ugly, For-Profit Troll Circus," *Vanity Fair*, April 28, 2017.

23   *"I'm not Inspector Gadget":* Eleanor Mueller, "Conway Denies Suggesting Wider Surveillance of Trump," CNN Politics, CNN.com, March 13, 2017.

24   *"there has arisen in the United States":* Dwight McKissic, "Resolution for the 2017 SBC Annual Meeting—Condemning the Alt-Right & White Nationalism," *SBC Voices* (blog), May 28, 2017.

24   *"We were very aware that on this issue":* Emma Green, "A Resolution Condemning White Supremacy Causes Chaos at the Southern Baptist Convention," *Atlantic*, June 14, 2017.

27   *"You've got to be careful":* Alan Blinder, Serge F. Kovaleski, and Adam Goldman, "Threats and Vandalism Leave American Jews on the Edge in Trump Era," *New York Times*, February 28, 2017.

27   *"trusted team of FBI agents to Israel":* "Exposing #Hoaxgate Black Propaganda & the False Flag in Hoax Jewish Bomb Threats," DavidDuke.com, March 27, 2017.

30–1 *"Despite what some of my colleagues"* . . . *"I hate the charge":* Laurie Goodstein, "A Jewish Reporter Got to Ask Trump a Question. It Didn't Go Well," *New York Times*, February 17, 2017.

One: Complacency

37   *"that supremely insolent Jew"* . . . *"were living in the forests":* Bernard-Henry Lévy, *The Genius of Judaism*, translated by Steven B. Kennedy (New York: Random House, 2017), 28.

38   *"We have, for the benefit":* Peter Stuyvesant, quoted in Bernard Heller, "The Jew in Early America," *Quarterly Review: A Journal of University Perspectives* 52, no. 4 (October 17, 1945): 313–318.

44   *"He is who he has been"*: Kaitlan Collins, "Trump Repeats Equivocal Charlottesville Rhetoric After Meeting with Black Senator," CNN Politics, CNN.com, September 14, 2017.

47–8   *"In isolated instances there is no prejudice"*: Rabbi David Marx, quoted in Anton Hieke, *Jewish Identity in the Reconstruction South: Ambivalence and Adaptation* (Berlin: DeGruyter, 2013), 151.

48   *"I have seen him in the office"*: Jim Conley, quoted in Ann Hendon, "The Leo Frank Trial: Week 2," *The American Mercury*, August 16, 2013.

49   *"Let no man reproach"*: Tom Watson, quoted in Steve Oney, "America's Only Anti-Semitic Lynching," *Daily Beast*, May 2, 2015.

50   *"THE NEXT JEW WHO DOES WHAT FRANK DID"*: Ibid.

50–1   *"Ballad of Little Mary Phagan"*: Lyrics found in ibid.

57   *"It would be inadvisable"*: David Weinstein, *The Eddie Cantor Story: A Jewish Life in Performance and Politics* (Waltham, MA: Brandeis University Press, 2017), 136.

58   *"Look, Franz, human beings in this world"*: Julius Streicher, *The Poisonous Mushroom*, translated from original German (Preuss, 2006).

60   *"Whether they like it or not . . . This despicable act"*: Dave Shechter, "'And None Shall Make Them Afraid,'" *Atlanta Jewish Times*, February 15, 2017.

61   *"You do not preach and encourage hatred for the Negro"*: Ralph McGill, "A Church, a School," *Atlanta Constitution*, October 13, 1958.

66   *"In an age where our economies are linked"*: Barack Obama, "President Obama's News Conference in London," transcript, *New York Times*, April 2, 2009.

66   *"I'm speaking to you in the center of a Europe"*: Barack Obama, "Obama Prague Speech On Nuclear Weapons: FULL TEXT," transcript, *Huffington Post*, May 6, 2009.

66–7   *"When a financial system weakens in one country":* Barack Obama, "Text: Obama's Speech in Cairo," transcript, *New York Times*, June 4, 2009.

Two: The Israel Deception

69   *"No matter one's politics or views on the Iran deal":* "ADL Condemns Vicious Attacks on Rep. Nadler and Iran Discourse That Has "Crossed the Line," press release, Anti-Defamation League, August 26, 2015.

70   *"Vitriolic rhetoric and threats":* Representatives Eliot L. Engel, Nita Lowey, and Steve Israel, "Engel, Lowey, Israel Statement on The State of The Iran Nuclear Agreement Debate," https://engel.house.gov/latest-news1/engel-lowey-israel-statement-on-the-state-of-the-iran-nuclear-agreement-debate/.

74   *"To stand against Israel":* Jerry Falwell, in *The Fundamentalist Phenomenon: The Resurgence of Conservative Christianity*, ed. Jerry Falwell, Ed Dobson, and Edward E. Hinson (New York: Doubleday, 1981).

75   *"It's hard to walk away from gas chambers":* Debbie Elliott, "Congressman Retracts Auschwitz Video And Apologizes, After Criticism," NPR.org, July 5, 2017.

81   *"just got back from the Middle East":* Dana Milbank, "A Not-So-Innocent Abroad: Trump Bumbles Across the Middle East," op-ed, *Washington Post*, May 23, 2017.

82   *"Through persecution, oppression, death":* Donald Trump, "Remarks by President Trump at Yad Vashem," White House press release, WhiteHouse.gov, May 23, 2017.

82   *"On to the second stop":* Marissa Newman, "On Plane, Tillerson Says Heading to 'Tel Aviv, Home of Judaism,'" *The Times of Israel*, May 22, 2017.

83   *"The Obama administration gave us eight years":* "RJC Statement on Pres. Trump's Address at the Israel Museum," press release, Republican Jewish Coalition, May 23, 2017.

84   *"Given that you are a Jewish student":* Adam Nagourney, "In U.C.L.A. Debate Over Jewish Student, Echoes on Campus of Old Biases," *New York Times*, March 5, 2015.

85–6   *"It was a flag from my congregation":* Gretchen Rachel Hammond, "More Than 1,500 at Dyke March in Little Village, Jewish Pride Flags Banned," *Windy City Times*, June 24, 2017.

87   *"created what some have referred to as a 'safe space'":* Tom Peck, "Corbyn Has Shown Poor Leadership on Anti-Semitism, Say MPs," *The Independent* (UK), October 15, 2016.

88   *"I note that two of the best-paid presenters":* Eleanor Rose, "Irish Journalist Kevin Myers Slammed for 'Anti-Semitic' Remarks in Sunday Times Column," *Evening Standard* (UK), July 30, 2017.

92   *"How American Jewish voters will respond":* David Harris, "A Jewish First Whether It's Trump or Clinton: Column," *USA Today*, July 5, 2016.

93   *"As the head of a religious organization":* Cathryn J. Prince, "For Trump, 'Religious Liberty' Could Mean Curtailing Freedoms," *The Times of Israel*, May 4, 2017.

93–4   *"As a minority faith community in America":* "Union of Orthodox Jewish Congregations Commends President Trump for Executive Order Protecting Religious Liberty," press release, Orthodox Union Advocacy Center, May 4, 2017.

95   *"It's unfortunate that some have sought to politicize . . . It would have been terribly unwise":* Harper Neidig, "Jewish Groups Divided Over Hanukkah Party at Trump Hotel," *The Hill*, December 10, 2016.

Three: The Unheard Thunder

98 *"My life would not have taken the direction it did":* Reeves Wiedeman, "The Duke Lacrosse Scandal and the Birth of the Alt-Right," *New York Magazine*, April 14, 2017.

99–100 *"From the beginning . . . we stressed":* Aram Roston and Joel Anderson, "The Money Man Behind the Alt-Right," *Buzzfeed*, July 23, 2017.

101 *"The attacks made on David Irving . . . as expected by an evolutionist":* Deposition of Kevin MacDonald in defense of David Irving (July 27, 1999), Biographies: Institute for the Study of Academic Racism, http://ferris-pages.org/ISAR/bios/Macdonald/depo .htm.

101–2 *"Among themselves they are inflexibly . . . There is, of course, nothing 'anti-Semitic'":* Samuel T. Francis, "Understanding Jewish Influence: An Introduction," blog post, National Policy Institute, September 24, 2004.

106 *"an army of sociopathic feminist programmers":* Milo Yiannopoulos, "Feminist Bullies Tearing the Video Game Industry Apart," *Breitbart*, September 1, 2014.

107 *"The controversy heralded the rise":* David Neiwert, "Birth of the Alt Right," *The Public Eye* (Winter 2017): 4–22.

108 *"A small group of Jewish philosophers":* Ibid.

112 *"That's one great trouble with our movement":* Quoted in Mel Ayton, "How Hate Groups Influenced Racist Killer Joseph Paul Franklin," *History News Network*, George Washington University Columbian College of Arts and Sciences, May 21, 2011.

112 *"We have to look good":* Lauren M. Fox, "The Hatemonger Next Door," Salon.com, September 29, 2013.

116 *"All the White people you meet":* Profile of Andrew Anglin, profile, Southern Poverty Law Center, https://www.splcenter.org/fighting -hate/extremist-files/individual.

118   *"Here's the plan"*: Brian Feldman, "[Very Surprised Voice] Those White-Student-Union Facebook Pages Are Probably Fake," *Select/All* (blog), *New York Magazine*, November 23, 2015.

118   *"White man, are you sick and tired"*: Keegan Hankes, "Eye of the Stormer," *Intelligence Report*, Spring 2017 issue, February 9, 2017.

121   *"In a heartbeat, words can turn into violence"*: Caitlin MacNeal, "Comey: Twitter Is Like 'Every Dive Bar In America,' But It's Free Speech," *Talking Points Memo*, May 8, 2017.

122   *"Step left if you know what's good for you"*: Dave Zirin, "A Lynching on the University of Maryland Campus," *The Nation*, May 22, 2017.

122   *"I want everybody to know"*: Crimesider Staff, "Portland Train Stabbing: Witness Recalls Victim's Last Words," Crimesider, CBSNews.com, May 29, 2017.

122   *"You call it terrorism"*: Matthew Rozsa, "Portland Stabbing Suspect: "You Call It Terrorism. I Call It Patriotism!" Salon.com, May 31, 2017.

124   *"My support has produced a much greater bang for the buck"*: Roston and Anderson, "The Money Man Behind the Alt-Right."

124   *"I think Trump was a legitimizer"*: Ibid.

125   *"If the Donald gets the nomination . . . Get all these monkeys"*: Profile of Andre Anglin, Southern Poverty Law Center.

126   *"The establishment and their media enablers"*: "TRANSCRIPT: Donald Trump's Speech Responding To Assault Accusations," NPR.org, October 13, 2016.

131   *"All Jewish surnames echo throughout history"*: Matthew Yglesias, "The ((((Echo))), Explained," *Vox*, June 6, 2016.

132   *"compiling and exposing the identities . . . can help you detect"*: Cooper Fleishman and Anthony Smith, "'Coincidence Detector': The Google Chrome Extension White Supremacists Use to Track Jews," *Mic*, June 2, 2016.

132–3 *"That's roughly the equivalent":* "ADL Report: Anti-Semitic Targeting of Journalists During the 2016 Presidential Campaign," a report from ADL's Task Force on Harassment and Journalism, Anti-Defamation League, October 19, 2016.

134–5 *"its support of Whitefish community values":* Tristan Scott, "Whitefish Council Adopts Resolution Supporting Diversity, Tolerance," *Flathead Beacon*, December 2, 2014.

137 *"is profiting off of the people of the local community:* Travis Gettys, "Neo-Nazi Richard Spencer's Mom Faces Financial Ruin as Montana Town Turns Against Her," *Raw Story*, December 17, 2016.

137–8 *"Put simply, the building has nothing to do with politics . . . Whatever you think":* Sherry Spencer, "Does Love Really Live Here?" *Medium*, December 15, 2016.

141 *"This rally crosses the line":* "World Jewish Congress President Lauder Demands Montana Immediately Ban Planned Neo-Nazi Rally: 'Alt-Right March Puts all of America at Risk," press release, World Jewish Congress, January 6, 2017.

141 *"Currently, we have 178 skinheads being bussed in":* Andrew Anglin, "World Jewish Congress President Demands Montana Shut Down Stormer Nazi March on Whitefish!" Daily Stormer, January 8, 2017.

143 *"My ability to do my job is gone":* Abby Ohlheiser, "The Man Behind the Neo-Nazi Daily Stormer Website Is Being Sued by One of His 'Troll Storm' Targets," *Washington Post*, April 18, 2017.

143 *"What right does the reporter have . . . I don't control my fans":* Mickey Rapkin, "Lady and the Trump," *DuJour* (May 2016).

143–4 *"You have to talk to them . . . I don't have a message":* Dean Obeidallah, "Why Won't Trump Denounce His Anti-Semitic Supporters?" *The Atlantic*, May 6, 2016.

144 *"We abhor any abuse of journalists":* RJC Statement on Abuse of Journalists from Presidential Candidates' Supporters," press release, Republican Jewish Coalition, May 24, 2016.

144 *"I don't hold black leaders responsible":* Jonathan Weisman, "The Nazi Tweets of 'Trump God Emperor,'" Sunday Review, *The New York Times*, May 26, 2016.

144–5 *"Abandon yourself to your feelings":* Victor Klemperer, *The Language of the Third Reich: A Philologist's Notebook*, translated by Martin Brady (London: Continuum, 2006), 99.

145 *"I would never kill them":* Colin Campbell, "Donald Trump on Reporters: 'I Would Never Kill Them, but I Do Hate Them',' " *Business Insider*, December 21, 2015.

147 *"As time went on":* Jack Moore, "The Reddit User Who Created the Trump-CNN GIF Is More Apologetic Than Our President's Ever Been," *GQ*, July 5, 2017.

147–8 *"We are going to track down your parents":* Keegan Hankes, "Daily Stormer Troll Army Threatens CNN Staffers Over Reddit User Behind Trump/CNN GIF," Hatewatch, Southern Poverty Law Center, July 5, 2017.

150–1 *"is sick . . . This country cannot defend itself":* Lili Bayer, "EXCLUSIVE: Controversial Trump Aide Sebastian Gorka Backed Violent Anti-Semitic Militia," *Forward*, April 3, 2017.

151 *"It's this constant, 'Oh, it's the white man'":* Emily Shugerman, "Sebastian Gorka said White Supremacists Were 'Not the Problem' Days Before Charlottesville," *Independent* (UK), August 14, 2017.

153 *"Is there anybody that doesn't negotiate":* Jeremy Diamond, "Trump to Republican Jewish Coalition: 'I'm a Negotiator Like You',' " CNN.com, December 3, 2015.

153 *"We are an incredibly inclusive group":* Jake Tapper, "WH: No Mention of Jews on Holocaust Remembrance Day Because Others Were Killed Too," CNN.com, February 2, 2017.

153–4 *"This is my pledge to you":* Meghan Keneally, "Trump Vows 'We Will Confront Anti-Semitism' at Holocaust Memorial Ceremony," ABC News, April 25, 2017.

154 *"Everyone's suffering in the Holocaust"*: Alexandra Jaffe, "Priebus: Immigration Order 'Doesn't Include' Green Card Holders, But Anyone Traveling to Banned Countries Will Be 'Subjected to Further Screening'," NBC News, January 29, 2017.

155 *"Given continuing incidents of anti-Semitism"*: "Cardin Writes to Trump as Jewish Affairs Positions at White House, State Dept. Remain Vacant," press release, website of U.S. senator Ben Cardin, July 5, 2017.

155 *"Now is the time that we have to make hay"*: Matthew Sheffield, "Alt-Right Activists Say Trump and Bannon Are Giving Them "Space to Destroy" by Keeping FBI Away," Salon, July 24, 2017.

156 *"The fundamental question"* . . . *"Americans, Poles"*: "Remarks by President Trump to the People of Poland," WhiteHouse.gov, July 6, 2017.

157 *"We deeply regret that President Donald Trump"*: Jason Le Miere, "Trump in Europe: First President In Decades to Skip Jewish Warsaw Ghetto Monument, Angers Rabbis," *Newsweek*, July 6, 2017.

158 *"For one thing, [it] means"*: "Charlottesville: Race and Terror," *Vice News*, 7:45, August 21, 2017.

159 *"It's been going on for a long time"*: Dan Merica, "Trump Condemns 'Hatred, Bigotry and Violence on Many Sides' in Charlottesville," CNN.com, August 13, 2017.

159 *"Many of those people were there to protest"*: Jennifer Schuessler, "Historians Question Trump's Comments on Confederate Monuments," *New York Times*, August 15, 2017.

162 *"What we may be witnessing"*: Francis Fukuyama, "The End of History?" *The National Interest* 16 (Summer 1989): 3–16.

Four: Stand Up or Ignore

164–5 *"Most Jews didn't vote for him . . . These are anxious times":* David Bernstein, "The Great Anti-Semitism Panic of 2017," op-ed, *Washington Post*, March 8, 2017.

166 *"These incidents need to be seen":* "U.S. Anti-Semitic Incidents Spike 86 Percent So Far in 2017 After Surging Last Year, ADL Finds," press release, Anti-Defamation League, April 24, 2017.

169 *"Racism is evil":* "Statement by President Trump," press release, August 14, 2017.

181 *"That the SPLC, of all organizations":* Andrew Joyce, Occidental Observer, April 19, 2017.

182 *"To be a Jew is to be a beacon of hope":* Rabbi Yosie Levine, "When the Cup of Wrath Doth Overflow: Violence, Vengeance, Vitriol and the New Anti-Semitism," 2017 sermon, https://images.shulcloud.com/634/uploads/Shabbat-Hagadol-2017-Cup-of-Wrath-Web-Edition.pdf.

188 *"a sharply declining non-Orthodox population":* Laurie Goodstein, "Poll Shows Major Shift in Identity of U.S. Jews," *New York Times*, October 1, 2013.

Five: Toward a Collective Response

192–3 *"Not being a sight-seer":* Kivie Kaplan, in "8.27—Selection from Oral History Interview with Kivie Kaplan, Regarding His Entrance into Civil Rights Work and His Election as President of the NAACP, 1970," *American Jewish History: A Primary Reader*, edited by Gary Phillip Zola and Marc Dollinger (Brandeis University Press), 320.

195–6 *"To the children of Satan":* David Morgan and Sarah Lynch, "Letter to California Mosque Threatens "Cleanse" Starting with Muslims," CBS News, November 26, 2016.

196 *"This is a war"*: Gavin McInnes, "This Is War!" Taki's Magazine, June 1, 2017.

197 *"They have to cooperate with law enforcement"*: Ryan Teague Beckwith, "Read Donald Trump's Speech on the Orlando Shooting," transcript of speech, *Time*, June 13, 2016.

213 *"The end of history will be a sad time"*: Francis Fukuyama, "The End of History?" *The National Interest* 16 (Summer 1989): 3–16.

214 *"Donald Trump will not set out to build an authoritarian state"*: David Frum, "How to Build an Autocracy," *The Atlantic*, March 2017.

214–5 *"As the subjects (thought they) shocked"*: Timothy Snyder, *On Tyranny: Twenty Lessons from the Twentieth Century* (New York: Tim Duggan Books, 2017), 21.

218 *"We do not subscribe to the view"*: Quoted in Snyder, *On Tyranny*, 23–24.

223 *"There is no quiet life for Jews anywhere"*: Arthur Hertzberg, *Jews: The Essence and Character of a People* (San Francisco: HarperSanFrancisco, 1999), 31.